Contents

INTERMEDIATE
information
TECHNOLOGY

JON SUTHERLAND & DIANE CANWELL

Hodder & Stoughton

A MEMBER OF THE HODDER HEADLINE GROUP

Dedication
To David and his family

Acknowledgements
The publishers would like to thank the following for
permission to reproduce material:
Life File (Figures 1.1.1, 1.2.2, 1.2.3, 4.1.2); Science Photo
Library (Figure 2.3.1); Security Enclosures Ltd (Figure
2.4.1).

A catalogue record for this title is available from The
British Library

ISBN 0 340 67946 8

First published 1997
Impression number   10 9 8 7 6 5 4 3 2
Year   2002 2001 2000 1999

Typeset by Fakenham Photosetting Ltd, Fakenham,
Norfolk.
Printed in Great Britain for Hodder & Stoughton
Educational, a division of Hodder Headline Plc, 338
Euston Road, London NW1 3BH by Scotprint,
Musselburgh, Scotland.

Introduction

Information technology systems are the main focus for the course you are studying, and under the general 'Information technology systems' headings, you will be looking at the following:

- the hardware used by various organisations, particularly those types which are industry-standard
- the software used by various organisations, again the most common and industry-standard types
- the information which can be stored in, sorted in and extracted from these information technology systems
- the implications for employees regarding the use and application of information technology systems
- the changing requirements for accommodation as a result of the introduction of information technology systems.

You will be covering four different units throughout this book, and each one follows exactly the performance criteria and range statements used in the course. We have given a series of activities which will assist with the building up of evidence for the portfolio, as well as end-of-element Assignments which cover all of the performance criteria in the element itself, as well as some of the core skills criteria. Because the course is so practical in nature, we have not always covered the performance criteria or range statements separately, but have combined them and given either an activity or an assignment which is either formative or summative in nature.

We have not given specific instructions for the use of any software or programs as this will very much depend on the applications available at the institution where you are studying this course.

At the end of each unit, we also give some sample end test questions to help prepare you for the unit test questions.

We hope you find this book a useful practical tool for the teaching and learning of GNVQ Intermediate Information Technology.

Jon Sutherland and Diane Canwell

element

Examine industrial and commercial information technology systems

1.1.1

Describe the benefits and limitations of commercial systems

1.1.2

Describe the benefits and limitations of industrial systems

In this element of the performance criteria, we intend to help you to investigate and examine different industrial and commercial information technology systems. Specifically, this will include looking at:

- the hardware being used
- the software being used
- the information being put into the computer
- the information being taken out of the computer
- the staff and accommodation requirements.

For the purposes of the assignment at the end of this element, it will be necessary for you to explain the features of selected commercial and industrial systems. The systems should be selected by your tutor, or alternatively by yourself and then agreed with your tutor. By investigating these systems you will be able to consider all the items in the featured range statements.

In a modern business, there are a multitude of different commercial systems which can be either purchased direct from a manufacturer, or, more commonly in larger organisations, specifically designed for their own purposes. In booking a flight with an airline company, a commercial information technology system will be used to confirm your booking and reserve your seat. In a hotel environment, it is common practice for the reception desk to have a computer system which logs the occupants of each room and tallies their bills for additional services. Even when you go into a shop, the cash register is no longer merely a place to store the payments made for products and services. It automatically registers the fact that particular products have been purchased, and this information can then be used to form a re-order to replace the stock.

Benefits of commercial and industrial systems

Simply buying a computer and switching it on will not bring benefits automatically. These benefits only come to an organisation if it takes the correct approach to the buying, use and cost of this computer. We look now at some of the more obvious benefits.

Accuracy

When an organisation has been relying on manual systems for the recording of its transactions or storage of information, it will obviously be concerned that this information be stored and recorded accurately. Improved accuracy will be one of the more obvious benefits when an organisation acquires a computer system. Naturally, the accounting section will want accurate information to work on, as will the managers when they analyse the financial data. Accuracy is particularly important when numerical data is being used and calculated, and an organisation will find that this is improved when changing from manual to computerised systems.

Decreasing costs

The financial cost of computerisation will always be a key consideration for any organisation. Each year the real costs of computer hardware and software are decreasing, though having said this, an organisation will have to realise that hidden costs are also involved. These different types of cost include:

- *direct costs* – these are the costs that can easily be identified from the beginning of computerisation, and include the following:
  - the purchase of the hardware
  - the purchase of the software
  - the cost of installation and cabling
  - the cost of staff training and development
  - the cost of time for staff familiarisation
  - the costs of maintenance and support contracts
  - the purchase of accessories

- *long-term costs* – these costs are a little less certain, but must be allowed for when budgeting for computer expenditure. They include:
  - maintenance and repair
  - the purchase of accessories
  - staff training and development
  - the replacement of equipment
  - the upgrading of equipment
  - general development costs

- *hidden costs* – as the name implies, these are unexpected costs which the organisation may not have budgeted for. In fact, they may even go unnoticed because the organisation will not be looking for these costs. Hidden costs include:
  - the cost of employing staff with greater skills and better conditions of service
  - the cost of time needed for learning new software or coming to terms with more sophisticated equipment

- the cost of buying computer equipment or furniture to make the users more comfortable and to comply with government legislation
- the cost involved in regularly updating and upgrading existing equipment and software to compensate for obsolescence
- the cost of insurance – although an organisation can insure its equipment, unfortunately it cannot insure its information; and it would be far more costly for a business to lose this!
- the cost of keeping in touch with changes in government legislation.

Efficiency and speed

Obviously, every organisation, whatever its size or type of activity, is constantly striving to be more efficient in the way it provides service to its customers. The acquisition of a computerised system for transaction-recording and financial analysis could help to make this possible. An organisation would be looking to improve efficiency and speed of operations in the following ways:

- *transaction processing* – because a computerised system can store, retrieve and process data much more quickly than can be achieved manually, it is not surprising that this can now be carried out more efficiently as well. It is, however, very important that the transaction be accurately inputted into the computer in the first place, otherwise the information will not be useful. In a similar way, once the information is contained in the memory, any amendments or updates that are made must also be accurate. Obviously, the computer will only manipulate the information which it receives, making it imperative that the individual responsible for inputting and updating the information be organised and accurate

- *speed of response to customers* – an organisation will find that it can offer a better and quicker service to its customers if it can carry out the following tasks by using a computer as opposed to relying on an individual to carry them out manually:
  - printing standard letters
  - printing customer statements
  - producing accounting information
  - producing management reports
  - monitoring stock levels
  - monitoring customer account information.

- *better overall control* – when an organisation relies on a manual system, many errors and omissions can go unnoticed until serious problems arise which might cost the business a great deal of money. Although there is some degree of error possible when using a computerised system, built-in checking systems can be used which will bring the errors to the attention of the user during the very early stages
- *larger volumes of work handled* – when an organisation records its transactions manually, this can be boring and time-consuming, particularly when it has to be carried out each week or month. A suitable computer system can speed up the process and eliminate, to some degree, the uninteresting activities for some of its employees. As a result, more work will be possible, and the organisation will find that what used to be lengthy tasks can now be quickly finished, giving the employee time to carry out more work
- *employees feeling more fulfilled* – because the employees are not having to carry out these tedious tasks anymore, they will feel a higher level of job satisfaction.

The impact on the environment

The impact that any IT system will have on the environment will very much depend

3

on the application of the system rather than on the actual information technology itself. Naturally, if the application is associated with some kind of pollution or other environmental issue, then any waste products which result from the process will have to be monitored very closely in order to ensure that legislation is being adhered to. For this reason, organisations that may find themselves in such a position tend to use monitoring systems and sensors to make sure that the levels of waste products are kept to a minimum and that signals are activated if maximum levels are reached.

Limitations of commercial and industrial systems

Costs

Obviously, there are likely to be some limitations to any system an organisation decides to use. The main limitations include the following:

- employees may have to be retrained in order to carry out their tasks, or they may have to be redeployed
- the initial costs of the system could be expensive
- the systems may have to be housed in special premises, and this may mean additional setting-up costs
- the organisation may have to wait a long time before it sees the benefits of the initial costs
- the maintenance of such systems has to be carried out by trained employees.

Security problems

It should be remembered that not even the most sophisticated information technology system is foolproof. Without careful management which would involve periodic backing-up of the data which is stored on the systems, there is always the risk of **data loss**. Not only this, but data can also be corrupted if the operator of the system is unaware of the implications of ignoring warning messages on the screen.

The other major security aspect is that of **confidentiality of information**. Obviously, if the system is open to a number of different individuals, then there may be a temptation to search the system for information about particular customers, clients or employees. Bearing in mind that the system may contain sensitive and private information regarding an individual, it is becoming common practice for systems to grant variable levels of access to different members of staff according to their position within the organisation.

Once information is on a computer system, it is relatively simple to make copies of that information which would contravene the copyright of the owner of that information. Given the fact that thousands of pages of information can be stored on a single disk, and that this information can be downloaded to disk in minutes, this issue becomes a very serious one. Data theft of this kind is only one new crime that can be associated with the wide-scale use of information technology systems.

Even if the data is actually secure within the system being used by an organisation, there is still the danger of equipment or software theft. Not only does this have serious implications for the organisation which has lost the equipment or software – since valuable information may be stored on hard drives and may be accessed by the thief at a later date – it also has implications for the manufacturer of the equipment or software.

Software piracy is extremely widespread, and manufacturers are torn between two very different concerns. First, they need to ensure that the software applications are easy to load onto hardware, and that the user can then follow a series of straightforward prompts. Second, the manufacturer is aware of the fact that, provided master copies are available of the software on disk or CD, it is very easy to pass the master set along to an unauthorised user.

(See Elements 2.1 and 3.4 for a more detailed discussions on security matters.)

Health and safety considerations

Although a computer is not a dangerous piece of equipment, there are several areas which need careful consideration when considering the needs of the user. Under the Health and Safety At Work Act 1974, it is the duty of the employer to ensure that his/her employees are working in a healthy, safe and hazard-free environment. The act which specifically concerns the user of a computer is the Health and Safety (Display Screen Equipment) Regulations 1992, and the main points of this piece of legislation are covered in Element 3.4 on pages 125–127.

The impact on the environment

As discussed in the previous section, the impact any applications used have on the environment will need to be closely monitored by the organisation. Legislation is in place which restricts the amount of waste products an organisation can produce and monitors the way in which such products are disposed of.

Explain the features of a selected commercial system

As we have already mentioned, when we talk about using a commercial system, we are specifically considering those used by some of the following:

- airlines – for flight bookings
- hotels or holiday companies – for making accommodation bookings
- retail stores
- mail-order companies.

Booking systems

A computer may be used for various booking requirements by various types of organisation. The organisations most likely to use their software for booking purposes include the following:

- *travel agents* – who will check with airlines for seat availability for their customers. This means they will have to communicate with the airline's computer system to obtain the required flight information and find out the availability situation. The airline company is likely to have a mainframe computer which allows on-line communication with each of the travel agents all over the country, or even the world, via the public telephone network. The travel agents will each have a **modem** which is connected to the airline company's network. Each time a seat is taken on a flight, the information contained in the airline's mainframe computer will be updated. This method of immediate updating of information is known as **transaction processing** (see Element 3.2, page 99)

student activity

● **COM** 2.1

In pairs, visit a local travel agent and find out how efficient they feel their booking system is. Having researched this, present your findings to the rest of your group.

● *hotels and some restaurants* – hotels will use booking systems in order to keep track of room availability. In addition, their booking systems will allow management to monitor the accounts of their guests and produce information related to room usage. Each guest will have a separate file containing the following information:
- their name, address and telephone number (or the name of their firm if this is paying for the room)
- the details of the room itself (such as whether it is a single, double, en suite, has a balcony, etc.)
- any additional charges to be paid by the guest (e.g. for telephone calls, room service or newspapers). Each of these additional charges will have a separate code which will be inputted into the computer together with the cost and the date on which the service was used

When the guest is ready to book out of the hotel, a bill can be printed from the computer which itemises each of the above.

Larger hotels which have several smaller hotels attached to them may have mainframe computers at their main office which can identify the availability of rooms at different locations should a guest wish to pre-book their accommodation for future nights in another part of the country.

● *libraries* – libraries also use booking systems for various duties they carry out on a regular basis. Some of the tasks which could be carried out using a computer program include:
- cataloguing and classifying – the information here can be updated each time a new book arrives
- the circulation of books – so that the librarian can carry out a monitoring process of the books being borrowed and of the date of their return
- the ordering of books and magazines (from publishers and printers)
- preparing reports – for the library's own use or for the use of other organisations, such as publishers
- dealing with enquiries – both the librarians and the general public can access the computer to search the database for information about the availability of different books.

student activity

● **COM** 2.2

Does your school or college library have any of these facilities? Research their uses and report to your tutor by means of a short memorandum.

Electronic funds transfer

Electronic Data Interchange (EDI) is an on-line communication system that links computers with mainframes. It can be used successfully in order to download geographically distant parts of a business to the main office. In this way, the central purchasing and storage facilities can be warned about impending requirements for particular products and other items of stock. Effectively, the branches can then request replacements from the distribution centre, and the distribution centre can then use EDI to request orders from its suppliers.

Networks similarly employ computers in order to facilitate easy communication between separate parts of an organisation. The computers can be used to request orders or re-supplies from the distribution centre. Another useful application of networks enables various authorised individuals to gain access to the stock systems and investigate the current stock levels in anticipation of their need for components and materials at a later date. In this way, these individuals can be alerted to deficiencies in stock levels and can request action to be taken in order to rectify the situation.

Electronic point-of-sale systems

Bar-coding is a system of recording data in such a way that this can be read instantly by a **laser beam**. Most supermarkets and many other retailers have phased this system in over the last few years. The vast majority of manufacturers produce their products in packaging which incorporates a **bar code**. Simply by passing the product's bar code across the laser beam,

FIGURE 1.1.1 *A supermarket bar code laser reader*

an individual can record the transaction. This allows the business to maintain accurate stock records.

Scanning bar codes in a warehouse or storeroom is becoming commonplace. Typically, there may not necessarily be a bar code attached to each individual item, but there will instead be a bar code on the shelf, or attached to the bin in which the item is stored. Employees can therefore remove stock from the storage areas and record the fact that it has been used by employing a portable **bar code scanner**. The information stored on these portable machines can then be downloaded onto the main stock-control computer. Again, the business will then have accurate stock information, and can act on this for reordering purposes.

Stock control

Databases are used extensively by businesses which have computerised **stock control** systems. Individuals involved in stock control are responsible for adding and subtracting stocks from the records in order to give the business a clear picture of current stock levels. In order to make sure that the relevant computerised system is being used correctly, businesses will institute a series of regular stock checks in order to identify discrepancies or inconsistencies in the recording systems.

Many of these computerised stock-control systems will trigger an automatic reorder once the reorder level has been reached. As we will see, this system is even more sophisticated when we look at retailers who use bar-coding systems which automatically record the fact that an item of stock has been sold, and then place this on an order which can be consolidated to the supplier.

One of the principal advantages of having a fully integrated stock-control system is that budgets and expenditure can be regularly monitored and controlled. Obviously, it is essential to the organisation that:

- the individual departments, divisions or sections of the organisation do not overspend their budgets
- orders not be placed if the stock required is held in another location (that stock could be relocated in order to fulfil another part of the organisation's requirements).

Since **budgetary control** compares actual and budgeted figures for revenue and expenses, all **variances** in the figures involved can be investigated through a regular monitoring process. This will enable a business to correct any problems or changes in the budget.

(See Element 3.2, page 103, for more on stock control.)

Order processing

Any organisation which buys and sells goods or services can use a computer program to carry out its **order processing** duties. Obviously, this will be a much more efficient and speedy process compared to having a clerk carry out this duty manually. An organisation will use its computer software to do the following:

- check that the goods ordered have been correctly supplied
- check that the customer's credit limit has not already been reached
- check whether the goods ordered are available in stock
- provide the warehouse staff with a 'picking list' of goods required to be despatched to the customer
- monitor the situation regarding any outstanding orders

- produce **invoices** which will be sent to the customer to request payment for the goods or services the organisation has supplied.

Each stage of the order-processing function of an organisation can be carried out using computer software. The degree of involvement will very much depend on whether or not the purchasing organisation also has information technology available to it. If we assume that it does, then the following can occur:

- The order can be sent to the organisation using **electronic mail** (**email**).
- The details from the order (e.g. the item(s) ordered, the quantity ordered, the unit price, the VAT, the customer status regarding any discounts, and the total amount of the order) are inputted into the computer
- From the information entered from the order, the computer will generate an invoice and, at the end of the month, a statement, which will automatically be generated and despatched, by electronic mail, to the purchasing organisation.

See Element 3.2, pages 100–102, for more on order-processing.

Payroll processing

As with order processing, **payroll processing** using a manual system can also be boring and time-consuming for the clerk involved. However, as most employees will agree, it is a vitally important task, and it is essential that it be carried out accurately and on time!

The larger the organisation, the more likely that its payroll will be processed by means of computerisation. A very small organisation may feel that it is not very cost-effective to go to the expense of buying a computer and learning the software involved for the sake of only a few members of staff. A large organisation, however, will have to ensure that the following information is available for each of its employees:

- the employee's name and address
- the type of employment (e.g. full-time, part-time, casual)
- the employee's payment arrangements (weekly, monthly or hourly, on commission or on a bonus basis)
- the employee's **tax code** and **tax rate**
- the amount of **deductions** (national insurance contributions, pension-scheme contributions, union membership fees)
- the number of hours worked in a particular period
- the amount of overtime worked in a particular period
- any bonus payments earned in a particular period
- any sickness leave taken in a particular period
- any holiday entitlement for a particular period.

The organisation will have the details of each employee stored on its computer.

Each week or month, these details will be updated for that particular period, and a payslip will be generated for each employee and issued to them. The details from each of the payslips will be stored by the organisation on a **payroll transaction file**.

The payroll transaction file can be used by the management of the organisation for the following purposes:

- to produce summary reports relating to expenditure of the organisation on wages and salaries, and to the number of employees. In addition, reports may be generated regarding absence through sickness
- to produce a **cash analysis** for wages and salaries purposes. This will be used to calculate the denomination of money required if employees are being paid weekly in cash
- to produce documentation for the Inland Revenue or the Customs and Excise Department for tax purposes
- to produce information to be used by the accountants when they prepare **annual accounts**, **balance sheets** and **profit and loss accounts** for the organisation.

Explain the features of a selected industrial system

In our homes, although we may not realise it, we have a range of industrial information technology systems – e.g. washing machines, dishwashers and central-heating systems. Out in the street, traffic lights and car-speeding camera systems are all examples of industrial technology systems. And when you take

photographs to be processed, an industrial technology system is again being used.

In a factory, systems are used in the manufacture of electronic circuit boards, bottles, cars and many other products. Without these, the flow of production and guaranteed quality levels could not be ensured by the manufacturer.

Streamlining and integration systems

In order to ensure that sufficient stock is held to cater for immediate production requirements, many organisations have prudently integrated their production systems with their stock-control systems. Systems which facilitate this streamlining include:

- *computer-aided design* – **CAD** aims to allow designers to store and retrieve their work. At an early stage, estimates can be made regarding the nature of materials and components required for this product. The business can then ensure, through cross-checking, that the stock either is in place or can be ordered in sufficient time for production
- *computer-aided manufacture* – the use of robots on the production line is one of the more commonly associated uses of **CAM**. However, a fully integrated system also incorporates stock-control and ordering facilities
- *computer-integrated manufacture* – this system enables a business to fully coordinate all production processes, from design through stock control to actual production. A series of sophisticated schedules and controls are incorporated in order to maintain flexible and efficient production
- *computer-numerical control machines* – using numerical instructions programmed into the memory, these machines are able to undertake a series of automated tasks during the production process. Typically, they will be programmed to produce a definite number of products in a single production run
- *manufacturing resource planning II* – this is a computer system which aims to coordinate the full production process. Essentially, it can:
  - translate **sales forecasts** into the purchasing requirements for particular materials and components
  - establish production schedules
  - produce individual work instructions
  - set deadlines.

The principal aim of the **MRPII system** is to maximise **capacity utilisation**. The system will be able to identify the fact that in order to meet specific deadlines, a business may have to request that employees work overtime. Alternatively, it may have to instruct the business to tell its customers that deliveries will be delayed.

Although setting up an MRPII system takes time, the business will find it invaluable since it will contain a comprehensive computer model of all the business's operations. The managers will be able to ask 'What if' questions, allowing them to experiment before actually risking any resources.

MRPII replaces the **MRP (Material Requirement Planning system)** which is still used, however, to calculate materials requirements for the completion of a particular order.

Design

Computer-aided design (CAD) packages are one of the most widely used commercial and industrial systems. The user can draw various shapes using the tools contained within the software. The software can also contain predetermined shapes and objects which can be imported from a master file.

Some CAD packages are used in conjunction with a **stylus** or **light-pen** to draw the design on the monitor. The following can be designed using this software:

- geometric shapes using lines, circles, curves, rectangles etc. Each design can

FIGURE 1.1.2 *Using a CAD package*

also be edited, and shapes can be 'filled in' with different colours/patterns. Alternatively, different textures can be added to the shapes
- two- and three-dimensional objects – which can be rotated, viewed and displayed in various forms.

Computer-aided design software can be used in the following areas:

- engineering departments and firms
- architects
- interior designers
- advertising departments
- television and film.

Process production control

When computers are used to control and monitor the production process, this is also known as **real-time processing**. It may be that a computer controls and monitors the temperature of a furnace or boiler and responds when this reaches a particular level by switching off the machine. Obviously, again, a computer can carry out this activity with much greater speed than

a human, and indeed this enables an immediate response. Because computers do this monitoring and control job so well, they are also proving to be very cost-effective to businesses. These micro-processor control systems have made the manufacturing and production process much more efficient, thus giving organisations the opportunity to become more profitable, as, for example, with industries producing the following:

- chemicals
- steel and aluminium
- food and drinks
- petroleum products.

The term **production process control** is related to systems which are involved in automatic control in manufacturing, the handling of materials and production processes of different kinds. Typically, a computer can be used to control any of the following:

- the process itself, by the use of **sensors** which can monitor input and output
- a heating system – e.g. in a dishwasher or washing machine
- data logging – for the collection and recording of production information
- quality control – by testing the products straight from the production line to ensure that they meet the organisation's quality standards
- the control of machinery – which we cover in the next section under **robotics**.

Robotics

The use of **robots** on production lines first came about in 1962 in the General Motors company in the USA, although the word robot is actually derived from the Czechoslovakian word *robota*, meaning worker.

Robots are generally used to carry out simple and repetitive activities, and are generally fixed in one position. However, with the onset of technological developments in recent years, robots can now be manufactured which are able to move in varying directions for various purposes. Some move along a track, either along the floor or raised above the production area, whilst others are housed on wheels or have the ability to 'walk'.

Obviously, the use of robotics has made an enormous impact on industry, and robots tend to be used to provide the following:

- *cost saving* – the initial outlay is enormous, but once purchased, a robot costs little more than using a human on a production line. And obviously, robots will not be absent from work due to sickness or holiday leave and do not have to take lunch or tea breaks!
- *speed and accuracy* – robots are capable of carrying out more tasks in a given time than a human, and they are also likely to be far more accurate
- *safety* – some of the activities carried out on a production line can be hazardous to humans. Robots, however, will obviously not be affected by toxic chemicals or heat from a furnace.

student activity

- **COM** 2.1

What situations can you think of where a robot would be useful? Discuss this as a group.

Features of a selected system

For this range statement, and for the purposes of providing evidence for your portfolio, you need to be investigating selected systems to enable you to consider the remainder of this element. In this final part of the element, we intend to give you some guidance on what software is available and what it can do for the user. You will then need to either visit local commercial and industrial organisations or use a case study provided by your tutor in order to explain about the one information technology system in the end-of-element assignment.

Word processing

This is quite a straightforward computer application. It can do what most organisations need for their business or administrative functions, e.g. write letters, reports and documents.

The **word-processing** package has replaced typewriters over the years as the way organisations produce their printed documents. It has several advantages over a typewriter:

- the text can be read through easily
- mistakes can be easily altered
- changes can be made without having to retype the whole document
- work can be stored for future reference
- work can be altered for a different occasion.

These benefits are particularly useful when considering very long and complicated documents.

Most word-processing packages will have the following valuable features:

- the ability to edit text
- help screens which show you how to carry out certain functions which are available within the package
- a spell-checking facility. This is ideal for someone who is not good at spelling. It scans the text and compares your spelling with a built-in dictionary. If required, the correct spelling can be

made to replace the error. Additions can also be made to the dictionary if required

- a thesaurus. This allows you to choose alternative words to the ones you have used
- a word count to count the number of words in the document
- a print preview, i.e. the facility to view the document before it is printed.
- mail-merge or mailshot facilities. These allow a standard letter to be merged with a number of names and addresses. This is very useful and time-saving for an organisation that would wish to distribute the same letter to several different organisations or customers.

Number processing

Another application area that has developed rapidly over the last few years is the computerised **number processing** facility. In this instance, the computer's role is that of a calculating machine. Software here includes:

- accounts packages, which normally offer sales, purchase and nominal ledgers, either as individual modules or as completely integrated packages
- payroll packages
- order-processing packages
- invoicing packages
- a fixed-asset register
- stock-control packages
- packages for job costing and the billing of materials.

Naturally, before an organisation decides to embark on a computerisation of the above functions, it is important that it clearly identify the areas that it needs to integrate. It will also need to identify the amount of activity undertaken within each of these areas.

Spreadsheets

A **spreadsheet** package is the computerised

equivalent of an accounts department's **ledger**. The name spreadsheet is derived from 'the spreading of the business's accounts on a piece of paper'. The computer user can enter numbers, formulae or text into each of the cells. **Columns** are the vertical sections of the spreadsheet, and the **rows** are the horizontal ones. A **cell** is one section of the spreadsheet.

This screen-based calculating machine allows information to be inputted in the form of text, numbers or formulae, together with the subsequent printing of the information. This information can be printed in the form of an exact replica of the screen itself, or in the form of a graph: a line graph, bar chart, pie chart or more complicated forms of graphics.

It is possible to change any number within the spreadsheet at any time, and the new results will automatically be shown. The ability of the package to carry out this function makes it a very powerful, useful and popular system.

Spreadsheets can be used by an organisation in order to:

- hold records
- depict their sales and costs
- determine what prices will maximise profits
- detail the costs accumulated for a specific job
- carry out financial planning and set budgets
- carry out tax, investment and loan calculations
- produce statistics
- merge spreadsheet information in order to show accounts from more than one department or branch
- carry out the conversion of currency
- carry out the timetabling and planning of staff.

We shall consider spreadsheet programs in more detail when we look at constructing a model in Element 2.3.

Databases

The term **databases** relates to what can be called an **electronic filing system**. In fact, most accounting software and spreadsheets are specialised databases. Most organisations will use and maintain a database in one form or another in order to:

- collect and store information regarding customers or clients
- profile products sold or purchased
- collect and store personnel records.

A database is a collection of **records**. Each record is structured into **fields**, and each field contains specific information. The desired structure and range of records can be flexible and can be compiled by the operator and, as such, is a formal way of storing information. A record will be a collection of facts about a specific product, client or supplier. It could also hold a list of sub-records regarding stock, prices and the number of units sold.

Before installing a database system, an organisation will need to ensure that the package is a suitable one. It will also need to decide whether a general package will suffice, or whether one more closely related to the activities of the business is required.

Graphics processing

The capabilities of a computer with regard to **graphics processing** will very much depend on the hardware involved, as well as on the software available. Because of this consideration, it is important that an organisation consider carefully the requirements of the application so that the correct hardware is acquired. This will avoid the necessity later on to upgrade the machine, which is an expensive option.

The **resolution** of the screen, i.e. the degree of sharpness of the image, limits the ability to display graphics of a suitable quality. **Desktop publishing** can make extensive use of graphics for **digitising** photographic images and for displaying a range of **type fonts** in different pitches.

Obviously, one major area of use for graphics processing is the design consideration of an organisation. Technical and engineering drawing can be carried out with precision and accuracy. In addition to the standard of work produced, the ability to store and subsequently retrieve and amend work can be of enormous value. Although graphics-design and graphics-processing packages can be very expensive, it will obviously depend on the business activities of the organisation as to whether it is cost-effective to install such a system. The following can be carried out using a graphics-processing package:

- computer-aided design (CAD)
- the design of stationery
- the production of simple pictures.

student activity

● **COM** 2.1
● **IT** 2.4

Apart from the short list given above, to what other uses might an organisation put a graphics package? Why would such packages be useful for this task? Discuss this in pairs and then compare your own lists with those of the remainder of your group.

Multi-purpose packages

Single-purpose systems, or the software used, tend to relate to independent functions such as word processing, databases, spreadsheets and graphics processing. Whatever application is used, whether it be a single-purpose system or a

multi-purpose system, the following points should be considered:

- does it do the job you want it to do?
- will it serve its purpose for a reasonable amount of time?
- is it compatible with the current system?

We already mentioned integrated packages when we discussed accounts and business applications, and **integrated accounts** is an obvious form of integrated application. To some extent, these integrated applications can virtually be seen as one single application as opposed to a collection of different applications. There are several applications available that integrate the individual applications – i.e. word processing, spreadsheets, databases and graphics – that we have already mentioned.

Many benefits can be derived from purchasing a multi-purpose or integrated package as opposed to a single package:

- all the computer requirement problems can be solved at one time
- it should prove cheaper than buying each application separately
- only one package has to be learnt, as opposed to several
- there is only one set of documentation to consider
- the key strokes or function keys tend to be similar throughout the different applications.

When using a multi-purpose system, it is possible to transfer information from one application to another. For example, information can be transferred from a spreadsheet or database file into a word-processing document.

Alternatively, a multi-purpose system can also have some disadvantages over the use of a single purpose system:

- it is not a specialist package, so no one

of its applications is the most sophisticated available
- for a person who is using the system for the first time, the integrated package may appear overwhelming
- the training time and the cost involved in learning all of the applications can be expensive for the organisation.

Of course, when we consider **information processing**, it is not possible to ignore the fact that communication both from within the organisation and from organisation to organisation has also been affected by the new technology available via the computer. The **Internet** and **electronic mail** (**email**) cannot be ignored here. The focus study given below should help to inform you of the dynamic influence these two inventions are having on the business activities of some of the more sophisticated and advanced organisations.

F OCUS STUDY

Information processing

The Internet may not prove to be such a threat to traditional letter-sending as people seem to think. Technology means new opportunities for the Royal Mail, but it also means new challenges too. Email is quickly becoming adopted by organisations, and is also spreading into the consumer world. For a few pounds a month, anybody who owns a personal computer and a modem can hook into the Internet and exchange unlimited electronic mail with more than 20 million other people around the world. These 20 million addresses include university students whose mailboxes often remain technically active after they leave their course.

Conventional postal services are now beginning to consider the long-term implications of a world in which email will be cheaper and quicker than posting a letter. They have already been losing business since the invention of the fax machine. On the other hand, some have their doubts as they feel that too little information or statistics are yet available concerning the true effect of email on industry. Email forms the bulk of traffic on the Internet and related electronic networks, but much of it consists of short and rapidly written notes which are passed from one colleague to another.

People also have different attitudes towards email, particularly when companies try to use it as a direct-marketing medium. Dataquest has used focus groups to ask computer users how they feel about receiving mail through an electronic network, and have found that they are hostile to the idea, particular in certain areas of Europe.

Marketing through networks is more likely to take place through advertising in electronic newsletters and virtual shopping stores than through direct approaches to individuals. It is expected that the next technological breakthrough for Europe is that post offices will move away from simple delivery services towards offering a complete service to commercial customers. A direct-mail company will create its entire direct-marketing campaign on desktop computers, compile its list of mail targets and then transmit the information electronically to the post office. The mail agency will then control the printing and assembly of the mailshot and, finally, deliver it.

assignment

If it is practical to do so, you could visit a local business which has either commercial or industrial systems in operation. Alternatively, your tutor may be able to provide you with case-study material which reflects the use of these systems. In order to address the performance criteria of this element, you must have some understanding of the benefits and limitations of systems which are in common use. In order to prove this, you should carry out the following tasks and present your findings in the form of a word-processed report.

task 1

Describe the benefits and limitations of two commercial information technology systems.

task 2

Describe the benefits and limitations of two industrial information technology systems.

task 3

Explain all the features of one commercial and one industrial information technology system.

element

1.2

Examine the components of a stand-alone computer system

1.2.1

Identify the hardware components of a stand-alone computer system

The term **stand-alone computer system** is used to describe a machine which is complete in itself and does not require any other equipment or devices to operate satisfactorily. In other words, this is a micro-computer which is not attached to a network or any other communicating device.

We are sure that you all already know that a **personal computer** (**PC**) is made up of the following hardware components:

- input devices – keyboards, mouse, sensor
- a system unit – this is the large box that the monitor sits on most of the time
- output devices – VDU, printer, plotter, sound
- storage devices – RAM, ROM, disk drives, tape drives.

FIGURE 1.2.1 *A stand-alone computer system*

We now intend to discuss each of these components in a little detail so that you can understand how each one contributes to the efficiency of the computer itself.

Input devices

A **keyboard** is one way of talking to the computer, and indeed is the most common way of doing so. A wire connects it to the system unit. The keyboard is made up of a QWERTY set of keys, with additional function keys, made up of the following:

- letter and number keys for inputting information and data. These are known as **alphanumeric keys**. Also include here are the Shift key (for capital letters), the Enter (or Return) key, the space bar, the Tab key and a Backspace key
- function keys for entering commands – these are the '*f*' keys which are placed either along the top of the keyboard or on the left-hand side. The specific use of these keys will depend on the software being used
- arrow keys for moving around the screen – these control the cursor (i.e. the flashing line) movement
- a number keypad – this looks like the keys on a calculator or adding machine. Included in this set of keys is the Num Lock key which, when turned on, allows you to use the keypad to input numerical information only
- the Ctrl and the Alt key – depending on the program being used, these two keys, when used in conjunction with other keys, allow the keyboard to act in a different manner
- the Esc key – again, depending on the program being used, it is possible to quit or escape from the current screen.

A **mouse** is also connected to the system unit, again by means of a wire. This is an alternative way of speaking to the computer, and some programs require the use of a mouse more than do others, particularly where drawing and painting is being carried out. A typical mouse has two 'click' buttons.

When using a mouse, it is possible to select different functions by clicking either once or twice on (usually) the left-hand button. Alternatively, the mouse can be 'dragged' to move something on the screen, select letters or words, or draw a line or shape.

A **sensor** is a device which outputs electrical signals when changes occur in the environment. Examples are heat, light, Ph, air, gas, sound and movement sensors.

The system unit

Also called a **central processing unit** or **main processor unit**, this is the brain of the computer, and it sends the instructions and information entered into it to the other parts that make up the hardware, e.g. the printer. Anything that is attached to the main processor unit is known as a **peripheral**, and this includes items such as joysticks, modems and keyboards.

The main processor unit enables the computer to carry out very complex operations. It contains **memory chips** which store instructions and data on a temporary basis whilst they are being used by the computer. Whenever software programs are being run, the program's instructions are stored in the memory of the computer.

At the back of the main processor unit are several **ports**, which are sockets into which the keyboard, mouse, modem, monitor and printer are plugged. At the front of the main processor unit is a slot into which disks can be inserted. This is known as the **floppy disk drive**, and it can be used to store information or to give the computer instructions about a specific program which may be being used.

A **hard disk drive** is also contained within this system. A hard disk behaves in much the same way as a floppy disk in that it can store information. Obviously, the hard disk drive can store much larger amounts of information than a floppy disk.

Contained within the central processing unit is a **motherboard**, which is a circuitboard into which the system components are plugged. The motherboard is connected to a **system data bus** which links it to its other system components.

The internal structure of the computer is known as the **bus architecture**, which refers to the way various components – e.g. the processor, RAM, disk-drive controller, and input and output ports – are connected to each other and communicate to each other. There are several different types of 'bus'. These include:

- *data bus* – which is for the transfer of data to be processed or manipulated within the machine
- *address bus* – which is the information containing the required destination of the data
- *control bus* – which carries signals concerning the various timings of the operations required
- *local bus* – which connects the processor with a peripheral and is used to speed communication with the **hard disk controller**.

Finally, the on–off switch can also be found on the main processor unit, usually at the rear of the unit, out of the way of 'little hands' or accidental use.

Output devices

The **visual display unit (VDU)** is also known as the **screen** or **monitor**. This looks like a television screen, and it is how the computer allows you to see what work is being carried out. The information which is displayed on the VDU is known as the **soft copy**, the **hard copy** being the printed version of this.

There are two main types of VDU:

1 *monochrome* – which displays a black against a white background or vice versa;
2 *colour* – which allows different colour backgrounds and displays. Colour monitors are more restful on the eyes, and also look more attractive.

Whatever the type of VDU, each can display differing resolutions expressed in dots per inch (dpi): the higher the dpi, the sharper the image.

The wide variety of printers available is sometimes overwhelming. It will very much depend on the type of information, and on the quality required of that information, as to which printer(s) an organisation chooses to have installed. Printers can range from relatively inexpensive **dot-matrix** ones (which print each letter or number as a series of dots) to the much more expensive **laser printers**. Laser and **ink-jet** printers give a much better copy and are also much quieter to use.

Computers which have **sound cards** also allow the user to input information through use of the voice. In other words, it is possible to give a computer instructions by talking to it.

Storage devices

Obviously, it is very important that any information or data which is inputted into a computer be capable of being stored. The different ways of storing information fall into the following categories:

- in the memory of the computer
- on disk
- on tape.

The internal memory of a computer is

measured in **kilobytes**. Each kilobyte contains **characters** (i.e. letters, numerals etc.) of data, and there are 1,024 kilobytes in one megabyte. Obviously, the amount of megabytes available in any one computer will vary. One of the many recent developments in computer technology has been the rise in the size of **internal memory** available. This falls into two categories:

1 **RAM (random access memory)** – when the computer is first switched on, the RAM will be empty, but it is used for the following:

- to 'boot up' the system
- to 'read' or 'load' an operating system from a disk
- to 'read' or 'load' from the hard disk
- to accept information from the input device (either keyboard, mouse or sensor).

Data stored on RAM is usually lost when the machine is switched off. RAM is made up of several **chips** which store information only as long as electricity is flowing through the system.

Two different types of RAM are used:

- *static (SRAM)* – which consumes quite a large amount of power and retains its information as long as the power is switched on. Although SRAM is quite expensive, it can be written to and read from very quickly
- *dynamic (DRAM)* – though cheaper than SRAM because it consumes less power, DRAM needs to be rewritten at intervals.

It is important for an organisation to know the RAM capacity of its computers so that it can find out if there is enough to enable it to run the applications required for its day-to-day business functions.

2 **ROM (read only memory)** – this will contain programs and data that the machine requires to allow it to start work. ROM is a part of the computer's operating system. As ROM is so important, a computer cannot function without it. The contents of ROM are said to be **hard-wired** and cannot be tampered with or changed by the software being used.

CD-ROM (compact disc read-only memory) is a storage technology that uses the same kind of disks that are played in a CD player. A single disk can store over 600 megabytes of information.

Hard-disk drives are internal to the computer and are often called the **c drives**. Some computers have an external hard drive which is connected to the computer by a cable. Hard disks can be different sizes and are measured by their ability to store information in megabytes. The hard disk is similar to a floppy disk in that it can store information, but it is never removed from the computer system

Floppy disks differ from hard disks in that they can be removed from the computer and stored in disk boxes for safekeeping. The floppy-disk drive can be used for the following:

- storing the operating system as a back-up in case it becomes corrupted on the hard drive
- storing software programs which have been installed on the hard drive as a back-up
- storing business information (which may also be saved on the hard drive) as a back-up.

The most common size of floppy disk is 3.5 inches. The storage capacity on a floppy disk will depend on the type of computer system being used, but generally it holds much less than the hard drive. The capacity of the disk will depend on whether it is single-sided or double-sided (this is known as the disk's **density**). The floppy-disk drive can read disks that are equal to or less than the drive's own capacity. A high-capacity disk drive can read low-capacity disks, but not the other way around.

Another device for storing information from a computer is a **tape**. This is very similar in its function to audio tapes. Tapes can work at very high speeds, and are used for backing up particularly large quantities of information from a hard disk. They are quite expensive, much more so than floppy disks, but are extremely reliable.

FIGURE 1.2.2 *A 3.5 inch floppy disc*

1.2.2 Describe the purposes of the hardware components of a stand-alone computer system

The storage and processing of information

As you will have gathered, **permanent storage** usually occurs on ROM. **Temporary storage** allows the user to delete data or files, and most commonly occurs on magnetic tape or disk. Recent technology has also allowed the use of **light disks** and writable CD-ROM. The **primary storage** of most data and instructions is, of course, held in ROM and RAM, whereas **secondary storage** involves the use of media which can normally be written to as well as read from.

Information processing systems may be either manual or electronic. Both kinds handle data, processing it in some specific way in order to produce an end goal. With regard to electronic systems, such systems comprise both hardware and software. The information-processing system itself is carried out by a **program**. It is useful to define these three key terms at this point:

1 *hardware* – this, as we have seen, describes the physical, mechanical components of the computer system, such as the keyboard, monitor, disk drive(s) and printer(s).
2 *software* – software is the predesigned computer package which provides the information and processes by which the hardware can handle particular forms of information. These are also known as programs.

3 *programs* – as you may have realised, programs are software, but are written in a complex computer language aimed at providing a flexible and foolproof system by which information may be processed.

Hardware functions

Let us now look again at the particular forms of hardware and how each hardware component interacts with the whole system:

- *memory* – often known as RAM (random access memory), it has five specific purposes:
  1 to store programs being utilised in the processing of data
  2 to temporarily store the data itself
  3 to store information awaiting processing
  4 to store information being processed
  5 to store information generated as a result of the processing function.

- the CPU (central processing unit) can be considered to be the real brain of the computer. It performs the following functions:
  – it monitors current operations
  – it ensures that all components within the system meet the requirements of the software in use
  – it carries out the arithmetic processing of data
  – it carries out the logical processing of data.

- *input and output* – in order for the machine to process data, this must be in a form which the machine understands. A computer cannot understand the same language that we speak or write: it has to convert all information into a **binary language**, after which such information is known as **input**. **Output** essentially translates binary language back into a format which is understandable to us. The computer converts the binary language and displays it, either on the screen, as sound or on paper (i.e. **hard copy**) via a printer.

- *backing store* – in order to fulfil many of the functions that are required, the computer must be able to file information. This information may be found in two places:
  1 *memory* – it is not practical or desirable to store much information here since it may be destroyed or overwritten. Certain computers do not have an in-built resident memory, and all files stored in memory are destroyed if the computer is turned off
  2 *magnetic tapes or disks* – an alternative location for the storage of information is on either magnetic tape or magnetic disk. **Datafiles** can be stored in these locations for retrieval in the future.

The basic uses of information-processing systems

Before we begin to look at the purposes of information processing in more detail, we should begin by looking at the basic uses of information-processing systems. The main considerations are:

- the receiving and storing of information
- the use of information
- the communication of information.

We shall look at these individually:

Receiving and storing information

A useful comparison to make here is between a filing cabinet and a computer storage system. Both have the following features:

- information is stored in a logical manner

- the information is readily retrievable, provided the user is aware of where that information is stored
- a system has been created in order to ensure that the right information goes to the correct place 'in the files'
- it is possible to update and amend information as required
- there is the opportunity to access and duplicate the information when required
- there should be a system by which irrelevant or out-of-date information is 'weeded out' periodically to ensure that the system is not overloaded with irrelevant details.

Obviously, the manual method of information-storing will require greater physical space. There is also the danger that important documents may be misfiled or lost. This is also true of computer systems. At a key stroke, a file may be accidentally erased or routed to an unintended location.

student activity

- **COM** 2.1
- **IT** 2.4

In groups of three, consider all the ways in which a computer could be beneficial in the storage of information. How would an organisation ensure that there is easy access to this information at all times?

Using information

A manual system can suffer the restriction of there being only one file in existence. This means that only one individual can have access to this file at a time. A way around this problem is to duplicate the file so that all interested parties may gain access to a copy simultaneously. However, this simply adds to the paper mountain, as well as to overall storage problems. Certain computer systems can suffer from the same problems. Unsophisticated computer systems may only allow a single user access to a file at a particular time. Equally, if the system is disk-based, then access to the relevant files relies on a number of disk copies being made. With this system, there is always the danger of one file being updated by a particular user whilst all the other users deal with out-of-date information.

Communicating information

There is a wide variety of communication systems. Some of the manual systems do have their advantages inasmuch as they involve, to a large extent, personal communication processes. Computer communication systems can, indeed, suffer from being impersonal, and give a sense of isolation to the user. Whether the information being communicated to a particular individual is routed via a manual or an electronic system, there is still no guarantee that the individual will read or even take note of it. To date, no system has been designed that ensures that the recipient does respond to information given. Certain computer systems will require the recipient to acknowledge receipt of the information, but this is really no more sophisticated than ticking a circulation list.

student activity

- **COM** 2.1
- **IT** 2.4

In groups of three, consider all the ways in which a computer could be beneficial in the communication of information, both within the organisation and with customers and suppliers. How would an organisation ensure accuracy at all times and also ensure that the information is secure and only accessed by those who have the authority to do so?

1.2.3

Explain the purposes of different types of software

1.2.4

Describe the hardware components required for different types of software

As we have seen, the programs that can be used on computers are also known as software. This term 'software' can be broken down into several smaller areas:

- *systems software* – which controls the overall operation of the different components which make up the computer. This software is usually supplied by the manufacturing organisation of the computer, and it helps a variety of different people to use the computer without having to know much about its workings. Systems software includes the following elements:
  - the operating system, which controls the computer internally
  - a variety of other programs which support the system, e.g. editor programs
  - **graphical user interfaces** which

provide a means of using the computer which can easily be learned

There are several important functions of any systems software:
- to allow the use of programs and software required by the user
- to make the computer perform to its highest capacity
- to help the user to get the best performance with program development
- to make the computer as easy to use as possible so that many different people can make use of it

- *applications software* – which includes word processing and the manipulation of numerical data. It is probable that the computer was actually purchased in order to make use of this kind of software. There are two main types of applications software:

1 *special purpose* – which is designed for a specific purpose, e.g. accounts or stock-control packages
2 *general purpose* – which can be used for a variety of activities, e.g. word processing

● *computer-aided design (CAD) software –* which includes the manipulation and creation of geometric shapes and drawings
● *scientific and mathematical software.*

Operating systems

The job of the **operating system** is to make the computer work as efficiently as possible. It helps to overcome the barriers which exist between the first-time user and the computer without taking away the efficiency and speed that the machine is capable of. The operating systems of a computer manage the following parts of it:

● the central processing unit (CPU)
● the memory
● the input and output devices
● the store facility
● the file control.

MS-DOS commands

Computers operating through the MS-DOS commands can be entered through the 'C:/>' prompt. From this prompt, the user can select from a menu the option required. This can be done through the use of a mouse or a keyboard. These commands control the various uses of the computer systems' resources, including:

● the management of the storage space
● the running of the applications
● the use of additional disk drives
● the running of different software programs.

These MS-DOS commands given to the computer from the 'C:/>' prompt are dealt with by the **command line interpreter**. Some are internal or resident in the memory of the machine, whilst others are called from a floppy disk.

Multi-tasking operating systems

Multi-tasking operating systems allow the computer to carry out several tasks in its memory at one time. The computer can achieve these activities by switching from one task to another. In this way, the machine is making itself more compatible with the working environment, where several activities are also normally taking place at the same time. For example, a secretary may be talking to a customer, retrieving this customer's record from the store and scanning the record for information, all at the same time. In a similar way, the computer will carry out these different, but related, activities concurrently.

File manager

A **file manager** allows the user to carry out the following operations:

● create back-up files
● delete files
● merge files
● list files currently stored
● sort files
● select files.

Each file is named when it is stored, and it is possible through the file-management facilities to call up a **directory of files** held either on the c:/> drive or on a floppy disk. Micro-computer systems also show the date and time a file was last used, as well as the number of bytes or kilobytes it has used. The directory will show the total amount of kilobytes used on the drive plus the number left free.

MS-DOS allows the user to create sub-directories for the storage of files.

Obviously this is necessary if the hard disk contains many files as it would then be slower and more difficult for the computer to manage a single directory. Whichever directory the user is working in is known as the **current directory**. The user will need to ensure that the file storage space is adequate before commencing work on a large file. If necessary, such a file could be moved into a sub-directory.

Graphic user interface

A **graphic user interface** allows a user to run several applications and carry out various activities. These are usually operated via a mouse and **icons**. The icons represent the different programs which can be run, and by 'clicking' onto the icon with the pointer of the mouse, the user can 'pull-down' menus to access the different and very varied functions available to him/her. Common software packages using graphic user interface include Microsoft Works and Microsoft Office. These packages are referred to as 'Windows', mainly because a series of windows or screens are available to the user, each having a set of icons with a pull-down menu available from each. Regardless of the application itself, all windows have the following:

- *a title bar* – which includes the name of the document currently being used or created
- *a menubar or toolbar* – which contains the icons available at the current time. When these icons are selected, a pull-down menu becomes available, and its contents can be selected as required
- *horizontal and vertical arrows* – which, when selected, will show the part of the document either above or below, or to the left or the right of, the central area of the screen
- *a Help icon* – which, when selected, will allow the user to identify the information available within the program to help them carry out a particular function.

The Windows applications available allow the user to operate many different types of program. Some of the facilities are common to all Windows applications, and having learnt one system, it is quite easy to move to another as the basic principles are the same for all systems.

Applications

Obviously, all organisations will require applications which will allow them to carry out both their day-to-day and their non-routine activities in an efficient and effective manner. However, there are certain similarities between all types of organisation when it comes to the applications they most commonly require from their computers. These applications include:

- accounts calculations
- payroll calculations
- stock-control calculations and functions
- management information services
- document production.

In order to carry out these tasks, an

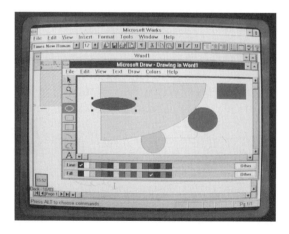

FIGURE 1.2.3 *Using Microsoft Works*

organisation will have to obtain some applications software (see pages 24–25 above). It can do this in several different ways, including:

- contacting a specialist organisation to write the program for them
- producing the program itself
- buying a 'ready-made' program
- buying the most suitable program and adapting it.

An organisation will need to take the following into consideration before deciding to do any of the above:

- the degree of urgency involved in obtaining the program
- the cost involved in obtaining the program
- the size of the organisation itself and the number of likely users of the program
- the equipment already available (or becoming available) to the organisation.

Data processing

It will be the case that an organisation requires a program to be capable of processing data of some kind. Data may be divided into the following areas:

- *structured data* – e.g. that which is inputted into a database program. We give you detailed information on these database functions in Element 1.1
- *documents* – e.g. that data which is inputted into a word-processing program. We give you detailed information on these word-processing functions in Element 1.1
- *graphics* – e.g. that data which is used with a graphic-design program. We give you detailed information on these graphic-design functions in Element 1.1
- *numerical data* – e.g. that which is used with a spreadsheet program. We give you detailed information on these spreadsheet functions in Element 1.1.

Throughout the remainder of several of the units of this book, you will be required to process data yourself by means of a computer program. In order to gain evidence that you are capable of carrying out this task with competence, you should complete the element assignments for each unit and retain the marked hard copy in your portfolio of evidence.

Controlling

A **control procedure** is the program created to operate a **process control system**. The procedure is designed to read the input data, process that data and send output signals according to preset rules: e.g. 'read the level of light, compare to the set limits and adjust the output if necessary'. A process control system is a computer system which automatically controls a process of mechanical device by sensing the need to vary the output. Examples of sensors are light, heat, humidity and pH sensors. A process control system is said to have **feedback** when it is the output of the controlled device which is first sensed and then fed back to the computer.

Modelling

Modelling involves creating a **computer model** which is a software representation of a real situation or system, and which can be used for an analysis of its operation. In other words, a computer model is a simplified version of a process. Good examples of modelling include the following:

- creating financial budgets with variable costs and profits
- the planning of journeys between geographical points using the roads available
- monitoring the queues at a checkout desk

- the control of traffic by traffic lights that monitor the number of vehicles and the number of pedestrians that pass along or across the road
- the production of a three-dimensional model of a building to investigate environment effects on nearby surroundings
- pilot simulation.

Modelling can also be used for the following:

- *hypothesis testing* – using computer models such as spreadsheets to test possible situations – e.g. financial break-even points for a business such as an airline or hotel – using 'What if' queries – e.g. 'What if we change fuel-consumption levels?'
- *gaming* – using computer software to model a situation for the purpose of a game – e.g. modelling a forest where treasure must be found
- *prediction* – using computer models to forecast a particular occurrence – e.g. the weather, or what is likely if a pilot makes an error.

We shall look at modelling in detail in Element 2.3.

assignment

This element looks at the hardware involved in computer systems, and should enable you to gain the knowledge and understanding required in order to undertake practical tasks in the remainder of this unit. Probably the easiest source of information about micro-computer systems and the availability of components are computing magazines, manufacturers' manuals and catalogues from stockists. These will enable you to make up-to-date comparisons of hardware and software in terms of performance. The format of the information which you will be required to show an understanding of could be in the form of a report or, perhaps more interestingly, in the form of a user guide to stand-alone computer systems. This assignment is aimed at giving beginners all the necessary information to determine which type of system they require.

task 1

Identify the hardware components of a stand-alone computer system.

task 2

Describe the purposes of the hardware components you have mentioned in Task 1.

task 3

Explain the purpose of different types of software

task 4

Referring to the types of software mentioned in the previous task, now describe the hardware components required for operating systems software, plus three different types of application software.

element

1.3

Set up a stand-alone computer system to meet user requirements

1.3.1 Identify the user requirements for a stand-alone computer

This element is a particularly practical one, and as such is progressive throughout, so we have not given you an element assignment at the end. The content of this element is related to the information we have given you in Element 1.2. In order to provide evidence for this element, you need to produce a specification which identifies a particular user's requirements for operating a stand-alone computer. In addition, you need to identify the user's requirements regarding hardware and software. Your tutor will assess the way you connect together the range of hardware items to ensure that it is compatible with applications software and is tested for all of the range statements in this element. You will not be expected to install the operating system or a graphic

user interface: this will be operable when the system is connected together correctly and powered up.

We very briefly give you a paragraph under each of the range statements to ensure that you are aware of the requirements for each.

User requirements and purpose

Your tutor will give you a scenario which explains to you what the machine is likely to be used for. This will include any details you require to enable you to propose an information-technology solution to any problem the user might be having. You will have to produce a specification identifying both the user requirements and the hardware and software needed to meet them. The evidence for this element will be an operational stand-alone computer which you have installed with the relevant applications software. You will also have to test the computer and make sure that the range has been covered for this element.

The type of processing activity and method of processing

Your tutor will make it clear to you *what* exactly the user will be processing and *how* they will wish to process that information. You may be told that they simply wish to use the computer for word processing, or you may be told that they want to use fully integrated software programs for a variety of different processing functions.

Identify the hardware and software needed to meet user requirements

Hardware

In Elements 1.1 and 1.2, we have already given you detailed information regarding the items which make up the hardware components of a computer. For the purposes of this present performance criteria you will need to identify what the user will need in terms of hardware in order to satisfy his/her requirements. Specifically, you will need to consider once again the following hardware components:

- *the keyboard* – whether this will be the main method of inputting data
- *the mouse* – whether the user will need to use a mouse in order to access software or carry out specific tasks using this device – or both
- *the VDU* – what type of VDU is required, and the choice of screen necessary
- *the main processor unit* – which will include the type of unit, the size of the memory, the number of ports required and the capacity of the hard disk

- *the printer* – which will include the type of printer, the resolution and the speed. Suitable types will include impact dot-matrix, ink-jet and laser
- *the cables and the connectors* – which will include the number and types of cables and connectors necessary in order to connect the main processor unit with the required peripherals; e.g. those cables and connectors used for power, the printer, the mouse, the VDU and the keyboard.

Software

An integral part of the decision you make as to the hardware requirements of the user will concern the software he/she will need in order to perform the necessary tasks. We have already covered in some detail the purposes of software in Element 1.2, performance criteria 3 and 4, and you may wish to refer back to this information before you consider specific requirements of the user.

Specifically, when considering user requirements concerning software, you will have to take the following into account:

- the *operating system* – which will include the efficiency of the computer and the management of the CPU, the memory, the input and output devices, the storage facility and the file control

- the *user interface* – which will include the link between the computer and the user, and refers to the way in which a person communicates with the computer
- the *applications software* – which will include the program the user requires, where they will obtain this program and how it will be used to ensure efficient and effective organisational activity.

Connect the hardware together

Install the applications software

Having connected together the different hardware components, you will be observed installing the software that you identified as being suitable for the user.

If the program requires a hard disk, the program must be installed before it can be run. Installing a program simply means plugging it in. Most programs have an **installation program** (which can be named 'setup' or 'install'), and this takes you systematically through the process. Obviously, the installation procedures will vary from program to program, but each will have its own set of instructions.

Part of the installation procedure is the **creation of directories**, which will demand whether or not you are installing through DOS (disk-operating system). Assuming that you are, then the following instructions will be used:

'DOS MKDIR' or 'MD' ('Make Directory') and then the name you want to give the directory
'c:' then 'Enter'
'cd\' then 'Enter'
'md' then the name of the directory.

This creates a directory with the name of your choice.

It is not possible to choose any name for your directory: it can only have eight letters or characters (just as with a file name).

As part of the installation process, you also need to **install the applications software**. This will be carried out using the instructions given to you with the program itself. In addition, you will have to **install drivers** (i.e. **print, display**) and **set up data directories**.

1.3.5 Test the computer system

The final requirement of this element is that you test the computer system you have set up. For the purposes of assessing you in this task, we have given you an activity at the end of this section which assumes that you are using a word-processing program as your software. This will help you to enter data, save the file, retrieve the file and print the hard copy.

Power up

Obviously, the first step in testing the equipment you have put together and the software that you have installed is to switch on the machine, having first ensured that your connectors and cables are all in place and soundly housed. **Powering up** can also be termed **booting up**.

Access applications software

Having powered up the machine, you now need to access the program that you have installed. To do this, you could either click on the icon you have installed, which gives the name of the software, or enter the name of the software when you have the 'c:/>' on the screen.

Enter data

In order to give you some data which you can enter onto the screen, you should carry out the following task:

student activity

Key in the following piece of work:

ALL ABOUT BEES

THE QUEEN

A colony of bees cannot exist without a queen, but it will support only one. The colony prepares a special cell for the future queen and, as soon as she has hatched, she will destroy any other potential queen cells.

A queen can lay up to 2,000 eggs a day during the height of summer, and most of them will become female workers. In the spring she will lay unfertilised eggs, which become the drones or male bees.

WORKERS AND DRONES

Three days after the egg is laid, the female worker bee hatches. Within a matter of days she gnaws her way out of the cell as a fully developed bee. She quickly gains strength and begins work cleaning the cells so they can be used again for egg laying.

The female worker is very busy collecting nectar, pollen and water to strengthen the hive. She may also guard the hive once her sting has developed sufficiently.

The drone, once hatched, can be distinguished from the worker by his size. He is usually bigger and stockier than the worker. His main function is to mate with the queen bee.

Save, print and retrieve

Having keyed in the work shown in the above activity, you should proofread it for accuracy and consistency of spacing and then save your work, ensuring that you give it a suitable file name.

You should also print one copy of this original file. Now make the changes required below:

assignment

Having retrieved your file, make the following changes to the piece of work:

ALL ABOUT BEES

THE QUEEN

A colony of bees cannot exist without a queen, but it will support only one. The colony prepares a special cell for the future queen and, as soon as she has hatched, she will destroy any other potential queen bee cells.

The queen can lay up to 2,000 eggs a day during the height of summer, and most of them will become female workers. In the spring she lays unfertilised eggs, which become the drones or male bees.

WORKERS AND DRONES

Only three days after the egg is laid, the female worker bee hatches. Within a matter of days she gnaws her way out of the cell as a fully developed bee. She quickly gains strength and begins work cleaning the cells so they can be used again for egg laying.

The female worker is always very busy collecting nectar, pollen and water to strengthen the hive. She may also guard the entrance to the hive once her sting has developed sufficiently.

The drone, once hatched, can be distinguished from the worker by his size. Usually he is bigger and stockier than the worker. His main function is to mate with the queen bee.

Having made the above changes, you should print two copies of the file and save it under a different file name, so that you now have the original plus the amended file.

element

1.4

Produce an applications software macro to meet user requirements

1.4.1

Describe the purposes of using applications software macros

This reasonably short element is linked quite closely with Elements 2.1, 2.2 and 2.3, where you will make use of **macros** to improve the efficiency of your practical work. We shall briefly give you information about the purposes and uses of macros, and then you will have to create a user specification for an applications software macro.

Macros are automated applications-software routines which may be created by the user and played back on entry of the required request. Typically, these routines include using single function keys to set a text to a particular size and type, or to save, print and close a file. More simply, this could just be to reset a standard tab setting, for example.

A macro is created by instructing the software to remember a particular keystroke sequence. When you need to use the macro, you simply repeat the keystroke

sequence and the macro is generated. When you want to repeat the same action again, you recall the macro, and this saves you the need to repeat the keystroke sequence over and over again.

Obviously, it is far more convenient and more speedy for the data-input employee to be able to identify particular keys or sequences of keys rather than to have to input large amounts of information several times. In addition to this saving of time and elimination of repetition, it is also very likely that the use of a macro will result in a reduction of error when data is being inputted. If several employees are responsible for inputting similar information in a variety of locations, then the use of macros will greatly eliminate the danger of error and go a long way to ensuring that information is inputted accurately, in the correct place and quickly.

Macros are a common feature of most

applications software and can increase the efficient use of a program. They may also be designed and implemented by management to make sure that standard procedures are undertaken and adhered to by each employee responsible for the input of data.

Describe the uses of applications software macros

Templates and batch filing

In addition to the repetitive keystroke sequences we have already mentioned above, **templates** can be set up for the input of data. These keystroke sequences and templates can be referred to as **automated procedures**, and they have two main advantages over the manual processes still sometimes used: speed of input and the reduction of error (both of which we have already mentioned).

All programs are likely to differ in the exact way that a template or macro is used, but they will probably produce the same result. We should also mentioned here **batch filing**, which is an operating system that allows the user to create files containing a series of commands that can be carried out consecutively. In addition, the programs allow the user to create directories and to display, move and delete files.

A template is a document which is used as the basic layout for other documents. This means that memorandum headed paper or the organisation's company headed paper can be stored as a template, and each time this file is retrieved an exact copy of it will be displayed at the top of each printed copy. The way the template is saved will depend on the program being used, but it is usual to save the template as a separate file and then retrieve it.

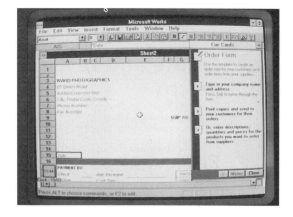

FIGURE 1.4.1 *An order form template*

As well as the headed paper just mentioned, a template can be created for any regularly used forms such as invoices, order forms, tax forms, reports and budgets. By using the template for forms, it is less likely that data-input error will occur as the computer will only allow certain information to be inputted into each particular section.

Setting defaults

As we have already mentioned, it is possible to use a macro to set a **default**. Basically, this means that the computer tells you that if you do not choose a particular option, then it will do so for you.

Calculations

If an organisation has a monthly bill that is the same amount each month, e.g. rent on buildings, then a recurring entry feature on the software can save time and prevent errors from being made, as the program will issue the same amount each time. By creating a macro, calculations can be made easily and quickly.

1.4.3 Agree a user specification for an applications software macro

1.4.4 Create and test an applications software macro

1.4.5 Review the macro and suggest possible further uses of macros for the user

We have put these three performance criteria together because they all relate to the activity which you have to carry out in order to gain evidence of your competence in this element.

You need to create a **user specification** for an applications software macro which meets certain requirements. You already carried out this task when you met user specifications for the stand-alone computer and software in Element 1.3, but this time you also need to design, produce, test and review a macro which the user could operate for a particular activity. Obviously, we cannot be very specific with regard to the nature of the macro as this will vary from user to user, but the following are considerations you need to bear in mind:

- **the applications software to be used** – you will need to know what software the user is going to install and what the program is being used for
- **the purposes of using the macro** – you will need to know why the user requires the macro
- **the uses of the macro** – you will need to know how the macro is going to be used and how often it is going to be used
- **the methods of executing the macro** – you will need to know in what ways the macro will be used
- **the data to be embedded in the macro** – you will need to know what information will have to be contained within the macro for it to be suitable for the user
- **the layout styles** – you will need to know what the macro is to be used for, and in particular which different formats of documents or column styles the user requires

- **the tests to be applied** – you will need to identify the ways in which you are going to test the macro for efficiency and effectiveness.

For the purposes of producing evidence for this element, you must create a user specification for an applications software macro which covers each of the range statements. In addition, as already mentioned, you must create, test and review an applications software macro. In order to prove that you have the knowledge required to carry out the above, you should produce a word-processed report.

task 1

In your report, you should describe the purposes of using applications software macros.

task 2

The second part of your report should describe the uses for an applications software macro.

task 3

You must now retrieve the macro that you created and suggest two possible further uses of this macro to the user.

End Test Questions

Text 1

Easytravel use a computerised booking system for their prospective coach travellers.

1 One benefit of the system used in text 1 is:

a any member of staff can take the booking

b coach travel becomes much cheaper

c confirmation of availability of seats is instant

d it may be impossible to book if the computer is out of action.

2 One limitation of the system used in text 1 is:

a any member of staff can take the booking

b coach travel becomes much cheaper

c confirmation of availability of seats is instant

d it may be impossible to book if the computer is out of action.

Text 2

An office supplies company is considering computerising its stock control system.

3 Which TWO of the following may be considerations which prevent the office supplies company from installing a computerised stock control system?

1 the expense of training staff to use the system

2 the increased efficiency resulting from installing the system

3 the cost of installing the equipment

4 the increased speed of processing the information.

a 1 and 2

b 1 and 3

c 3 and 4

d 1 and 4.

4 Which TWO of the following might be reasons why the office supplies company may be persuaded to install the computerised stock control system?

1 the expense of training staff to use the system
2 the increased efficiency resulting from installing the system
3 the cost of installing the equipment
4 the increased speed of processing the information.
  a 1 and 2
  b 1 and 4
  c 2 and 4
  d 2 and 3.

5 One major benefit to a manufacturing organisation of using robotics is:

  a more staff would need to be employed
  b the cost of production would be increased
  c less faults would be encountered during the process
  d staff training would be required.

6 One major disadvantage to a manufacturing organisation of using robotics is:

  a more staff would need to be employed
  b the cost of production would be increased
  c less faults would be encountered during the process
  d staff training would be required.

Questions 7 and 8 are related to Text 3.

Text 3

One major organisation uses floppy disks to store all their computer-aided design material.

7 One problem of using floppy disks for storage of computer-aided design is:

  a ease of access for amendment

  b security and confidentiality of material
  c less accurate information
  d less attractive designs.

8 One benefit of using floppy disks for storage of computer-aided design is:

  a ease of access for amendment
  b security and confidentiality of material
  c less accurate information
  d less attractive designs.

Questions 9 and 10 relate to Figures 1, 2 and 3.

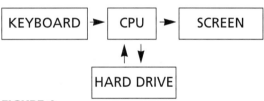

FIGURE 1

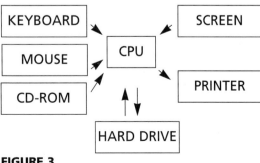

FIGURE 2

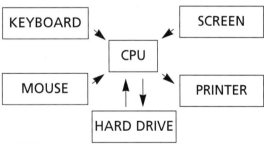

FIGURE 3

9 Which of the figures on page 39 has only one input device?

  a Figure 1
  b Figure 2
  c Figure 3.

10 Which of the figures on page 39 has only one output device?

  a Figure 1
  b Figure 2
  c Figure 3.

11 What is the main purpose of a CD-ROM?

  a to store information
  b to input information
  c to output information
  d to process information.

Questions 12 to 14 are related to Figure 4.

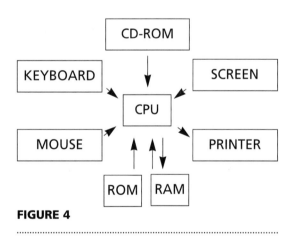

FIGURE 4

12 What is the purpose of the ROM and RAM?

  a to process
  b as a memory
  c as an output device
  d as an input device.

13 Which of the following is used as an input device?

  a ROM
  b mouse
  c plotter
  d screen.

14 Which of the following is used as an output device?

  a ROM
  b mouse
  c plotter
  d screen.

15 Which TWO of the following are the main purposes of operating systems software?

  1 file management
  2 system control
  3 manipulation of numerical data
  4 graphic design.
    a 1 and 2
    b 2 and 3
    c 3 and 4
    d 1 and 4.

16 Which of the following can be used to permanently store information?

  a a VDU
  b a CD-ROM
  c a CPU
  d RAM.

17 Which TWO of the following are the main purposes of applications software?

  1 file management
  2 system control
  3 manipulation of numerical data
  4 graphic design.
    a 1 and 2
    b 2 and 3
    c 3 and 4
    d 1 and 4.

18 Which of the following is an essential
hardware component of a spreadsheet
system?

a a printer
b a plotter
c a sensor
d a mouse.

19 Which of the following is an essential
component of a system used by a word
processing operator?

a a plotter
b a mouse
c a sensor
d a printer.

20 Which TWO of the following are good
examples of modelling?

1 pilot simulation
2 journey planning
3 word processing
4 databases.
    a 1 and 2
    b 2 and 3
    c 3 and 4
    d 1 and 4.

21 An installation program can be named
as which two of the following?

1 drivers
2 setup
3 install
4 display.
    a 1 and 2
    b 2 and 3
    c 3 and 4
    d 1 and 4.

22 In which of the following should work
be saved?

a working directory
b system directory
c applications directory
d drivers directory.

23 Which of the following should be the
initial check to ensure safe and accurate
installation of a stand-alone computer
system?

a print facility
b save facility
c power up
d accessing of software.

24 What is the main purpose of a macro?

a to increase the profits of the
     organisation
b to increase speed of operation
c to improve the corporate image of
     the organisation
d to evaluate software.

25 The main benefit of using a macro is:

a to reduce data entry errors
b to evaluate software
c to set up tables
d to draw graphs.

26 Which TWO of the following would be
suitable for using a template?

1 to set up a table
2 to set up a standard letter
3 to draw graphs
4 to evaluate software.
    a 1 and 2
    b 2 and 3
    c 3 and 4
    d 1 and 4.

27 When a macro is used for automated
procedures, which TWO of the
following are their main advantages?

1 improve corporate image
2 improve organisation's profit
   margin
3 speed of input
4 reduction of error.
    a 1 and 2
    b 2 and 3
    c 3 and 4
    d 1 and 4.

Questions 28 to 30 are related to Text 4.

Text 4

An organisation has decided to process its orders to suppliers by computer and to produce a series of macros.

28 Which of the following items on the order could be input by use of a macro?

  a the quantity ordered
  b the description of the item ordered
  c the name and address of the supplier
  d the price of the item ordered.

29 The organisation has written another macro which allocates the next order number. Which of the following would need to be written into the user specification?

  a the name and address of the organisation
  b the name and address of the supplier
  c the next available order number
  d the data.

30 If the organisation wanted to produce address labels for the envelopes in which the orders are posted, which of the following would have to be written into the user specification of this macro?

  a the date
  b the organisation's name
  c the order number
  d the key sequence required to produce the label.

element

2.1

Process commercial documents

2.1.1 Describe types of commercial document

The term **commercial documents** simply relates to any pieces of paper which are in regular use within an organisation. This can include the purchase, sales, payment and receipt documents, but also documents such as letters, memos, invitations and notices. We intend to deal with some of these documents individually.

Agenda

An **agenda** (see Figure 2.1.1) gives the date, time and venue of a meeting. It also itemises the programme of business which the meeting wishes to discuss. The first three items – apologies for absence, the minutes of the last meeting, and matters arising from the minutes of the last meeting – are very general and appear on an agenda for any kind of meeting.

A **chairperson's agenda** will contain more information than the ordinary agenda. Here also, space will be left on the right-hand side of the page so that the Chairperson can make notes during the meeting.

Business letter

A **business letter** can be sent by an organisation to deal with many differing occurrences. Unlike a memorandum (which we look at a little later), a business letter will be sent outside the organisation. It is important therefore that it be neat, accurate and well-presented.

The headed paper used by the organisation for its business letters (see, for example, Figure 2.1.2) forms part of its **corporate image** as it gives the information

CHEDISTON SOUTH SAFETY REPRESENTATIVES MEETING

A meeting of Safety Representatives will be held in the Conference Centre on Friday 23 June, 19.. at 0930.

AGENDA

1 Apologies for absence.

2 Minutes of the last meeting.

3 Matters arising from the minutes.

4 Report from the Chief Safety Officer on recent legislation received on Health and Safety at Work procedures.

5 Consider implications of possible new extension to the office block.

6 Feedback report from those who recently attended the training sessions at Head Office.

7 Any other business.

8 Date of next meeting.

SARAH BROWN
Secretary

FIGURE 2.1.1 *An example of the way an agenda would be prepared*

Gillette U.K. Ltd.
North Atlantic Group
Great West Road, Isleworth
Middlesex TW7 5NP England
Telephone 0181 560 1234
Fax 0181 847 6165

Gillette

5 March 1996

Mr Jon Sutherland
Sutherland And Canwell
The Old Post Office
Walpole
Suffolk
IP19 9AF

Dear Mr Sutherland,

Thank you for your letter from which I am pleased to learn of the interest you take in our company.

I regret that we do not have the facilities to answer your specific questions however, I am enclosing a copy of our Company annual report and relative leaflets which I hope will be of help to you with your project.

Yours sincerely,

Imelda Quinn

IMELDA QUINN
CONSUMER RELATIONS DEPARTMENT

A Subsidiary of
The Gillette Company

Registered Office.
Gillette Corner
Great West Road
Isleworth Middlesex TW7 5NP

Registered in England
Under Registration
No. 254912

FIGURE 2.1.2 *An example of company headed paper used to send out business letters*

an organisation would wish each of its customers or clients to see regularly, namely:

- the name and address of the organisation
- the telephone number, fax number and/or telex number of the organisation
- the registered address of the organisation, as this may be different from its postal address
- the company registration number
- the names of the directors of the organisation
- any other companies the organisation may represent or be affiliated to.

The layout or format of the business letter will usually also be part of the organisation's corporate image, and different organisations have their own rules about the way in which a letter should be displayed. It is common nowadays to use the fully-blocked method of display, which means that each part of the letter commences at the left-hand margin.

The following format can be used as a guideline:

- *our reference* – this can be initials and/or numbers which the organisation sending the letter will use for filing purposes
- *your reference* – this again is usually initials and/or numbers which the organisation receiving the letter has used in previous correspondence
- *the date* – all letters must be dated
- *the name and address of the recipient* (the person or organisation to which the letter is being sent) – when using the fully-blocked style of business letter, it is normal to use **open punctuation** in this section. This means that no punctuation is required in the name and address
- *the name of the town* – in capitals, with the postcode on a line of its own
- *the salutation* – this is the 'Dear Sir/Madam/Mr ... /Mrs ... /Miss ...' etc
- *the heading* – very often, after the 'Dear Sir/etc.', an organisation will give the letter a title. This is normally typed either in capitals or with initial capital letters only, and may be underlined or emboldened
- *the body of the letter* – each line of the paragraph commences on the left-hand margin, and a line space is left between paragraphs
- *the complimentary close* – this is the 'Yours faithfully' or 'Yours sincerely'. The complimentary close will match the salutation. When using 'Dear Sir/Madam', 'Yours faithfully' is used. When using 'Dear Mr/etc.', 'Yours sincerely' is used at the end
- *the name of the person signing the letter, as well as their title* – this is typed in after allowing space for a signature
- *enclosure(s)* – any enclosed additional information which is mentioned in the body of the letter is usually indicated at the foot of the letter. This is done by typing 'Enc(s)' after the complimentary close.

Invoice

A few days after the receipt of goods ordered and delivered (or sometimes with the goods), an organisation will receive an **invoice** which states the quantity, description, unit price, total price and VAT content of the order. The invoice will also list the **gross value** of the order, less any **discounts**, plus the invoice total. (See Figure 2.1.3.)

Memorandum

Internal **memoranda** are used for communication between different departments within the same organisation. These are often called **memos**. A memo is normally shorter than a business letter and usually deals with one particular subject. When more than one point is being made, it is normal to number them. Memos are not signed in the same way as a business letter, but the person issuing the memo will often initial it at the end.

Minutes

Minutes must be taken at each meeting held when an agenda has been prepared for the meeting. It is the role of the **minutes secretary** to 'take' the minutes (either in shorthand or in longhand) and to type these up after the meeting (see Figure

TO Sothereland and Conwell		NUMBER	5/149/dec

TO Sothereland and Conwell	NUMBER	5/149/dec
	DATE	28/2/..
	TERMS	2.5%
YOUR ORDER NO ST445	DISPATCH DATE	30/1/..

QUANTITY	DESCRIPTION	UNIT PRICE	TOTAL PRICE	VAT
14 reams	A4 A54 white A4 paper	£3.01	£42.03	£7.35
10 boxes	D11 envelopes	£2.00	£20.00	£3.50
	Gross Value	£62.03		
	LESS Trade Discount	£1.55		
	Net Value of Goods	£60.48		
	PLUS VAT @ 17.5%	£10.85		
	INVOICE TOTAL	£71.33		

FIGURE 2.1.3 *An example of a completed invoice*

2.1.4). These minutes are then distributed to those attending the meeting, and a copy is filed. At the next meeting, the minutes will be read under item 2 of the agenda, and anything which needs reporting on as a result of the minutes will be dealt with under item 3.

When taking minutes at a meeting, the secretary should remember the following points:

- minutes should be written in the third person and in the past tense (e.g. 'Mr Smith reported that that the training session had been a success.')
- make sure you state clearly what was said during the meeting so that it is obvious what decisions were made
- be brief: there is no need to write every word that was said, just an outline
- type the minutes in the same order as the agenda for the meeting.

CHEDISTON SOUTH SAFETY REPRESENTATIVES MEETING

A meeting of Safety Representatives was held in the Conference Centre on Friday 23 June 19.. at 0930.

Present   Ms B Mills (in the Chair)
               Mr P Taylor
               Mr S Parsons
               Mr H Arfield
               Ms P Olivier
               Mr S Brenner

               Miss S Brown (Secretary)

1 **APOLOGIES**
   Apologies were received from Mr P Kane who was attending the Safety Seminar at Head Office.

2 **MINUTES OF LAST MEETING**
   The minutes of the previous meeting were read and signed as being a true record.

3 **MATTERS ARISING**
   There were no matters arising from the previous minutes.

4 **REPORT FROM THE CHIEF SAFETY OFFICER**
   Ms Mills reported that the recent Government legislation concerning Health and Safety at Work procedures would require some careful consideration.

   The new procedures would be copied and distributed to all concerned. Ms Mills stated that she would like a sub-committee to be formed to study the legislation and report back at the next meeting.

   Mr Taylor, Mr Brenner and Ms Olivier volunteered to form the sub-committee, and agreed to meet on Tuesday 27 June 19..

5 **IMPLICATIONS OF POSSIBLE NEW EXTENSION TO THE OFFICE BLOCK**
   Ms Olivier reported that she had seen the plans for the new office block and was concerned that not enough space had been allocated to each member of staff using that block.

   After some discussion it was decided that Ms Mills would speak to the architects and report her findings to the next meeting.

6 **REPORT ON RECENT TRAINING SESSIONS**
   It was generally felt that the training sessions were of value, and that they should continue. Mr Kane was attending his session at the present time, and once Ms Olivier had attended, then all staff had been involved. It was anticipated that these sessions would take place annually, and that all representatives should ensure they attend.

7 **ANY OTHER BUSINESS**
   Mr Parsons reported that there had been some problems with the installation of the new electronic typewriters. The location of some of the machines had meant that wires were trailing in a dangerous way. Mr Parsons had dealt with this problem and all now seemed to be working well and safely.

8 **DATE OF NEXT MEETING**
   The date of the next meeting was set for Friday 27 July 19.. at 0930. The venue will be arranged.

....
Signed

FIGURE 2.1.4 *An example of the way the minutes of a meeting would be presented*

Newsletter

Another way that an organisation can notify all of its employees about interesting and informative facts is by issuing a **newsletter**. Several larger organisations use newsletters to contact all members of staff, particularly where such organisations have different branches around the UK. These newsletters can include both formal and informal information. They may state the fact that a director is retiring, or, in fact, that one of the sales assistants has recently given birth to a baby.

Report

Although **reports** issued or received by an organisation can be either informal or very formal, both types contain certain common elements, though not necessarily the same format.

A report may contain research which has been carried out for a specific purpose. Or it may be an account of something which has taken place and been reported on. At any rate, a report will contain the following headings:

- *terms of reference* – this will state what you have been asked to do. It may be that you have been asked to conduct research on a particular aspect or topic
- *procedure* – this will say how you have gone about gathering the information you are stating
- *findings* – in this section, you will state what facts you have found out. You will

not make statements about your recommendations at this stage but will simply state facts instead
- *conclusion* – this will be a general statement about your findings. Again, this is not the place to make recommendations, it is where you will sum up your findings
- *recommendations* – on the basis of your findings and conclusions, you will make recommendations for future research or projects.

It is usual to sign and date a report. Sometimes, it is helpful to break down the headings used in a report. This could be done by using a series of numbers, for example:

1 Establishment of company catering facilities
  (a) Lunch period arrangements
    (i) Arrangements of seating

student activity

- ● **COM** 2.2
- ● **IT** 2.1, 2.2

Compile a report on the effectiveness of different forms of commercial document. In this report, you should include all the advantages and disadvantages of the different forms, as well as the features of each communication type. You should use the correct report format, which should be word-processed.

Create templates with appropriate page attributes and layouts

This element is linked to the previous two when you investigated and then produced applications software macros. You need to be able to create a template which takes into account each of the items in the set of range statements.

We will give you a paragraph under each of the range statements so that you are aware what each of the statements relates to.

Page attributes

It is possible, with the software now available, to change the attributes of a page in very simple ways. By **page attributes** we mean the **orientation** and the **paper size**. The orientation refers to the way the printer will deal with the copy required. By selecting the page set-up or the printer set-up in Windows, for example, it is very easy to select the orientation and then click on the 'portrait' or 'landscape' icons. Portrait means that the short side of the edge of the A4 paper is at the top of the document, and landscape means that the wider side is at the top (see Figure 2.1.5). It is easy to remember which is which by thinking of a picture hanging on a wall: portrait of somebody would normally be deeper than it is wide, whereas a landscape painting would be wider than it is deep. Once this orientation has been selected, it will remain throughout the document until you wish to change it again. This means that it is possible to change from portrait to landscape on different pages of a document if required.

Portrait paper

Landscape paper

FIGURE 2.1.5 *Portrait and landscape paper*

Layouts

The layout of a document refers to the way you wish the finished copy to look. It is possible with all word-processing software to **format** the document, and as we have already seen, this can refer to the orientation or page attributes, or to the layout desired.

Column layouts

It is very easy to make a document look like a magazine, newsletter or newspaper

The term 'database' relates to what can be called an electronic filing system. In fact, most accounting software and spreadsheets are specialised databases. Most organisations would use and maintain a database in one form or another in order to:

- collect and store information regarding customers or clients

- to profile products sold or purchased

- to collect and store personnel records.

A database is a collection of records. Each record is structured into fields and each field contains specific information. The desired structure and range of records can be flexible and can be compiled by the operator and, as such, is a formal way of storing information. The record would be a collection of facts about a specific product, client or supplier.

It could also hold a list of records regarding stock, prices and number of units sold.

Before embarking on the installation of a database system, the organisation would need to ensure that the package would be suitable. In addition, it would need to decide whether a general package would suffice or whether a more closely related one to the activities of the business were required.

Spreadsheets, on the other hand, deal with numerical data and the software is capable of manipulating this information as and when required. Spreadsheet information is input into the program using a series of the following:

> columns
> rows
> cells.

When the information is being keyed in then one cell is highlighted and this is said to be the 'active cell'.

Word processing deals very much with text and works on a much more superior principle than that of the typewriter. All the same skills used in typewriting are required in word processing, together with the knowledge required to understand the use of each of the function keys on the keyboard.

STUDENT INFORMATION

64

FIGURE 2.1.6 *An example of column printing*

with two columns of text on each page. When you select multiple columns at the commencement of the work, the software will continue to use this layout until the end of the document or until you select otherwise. You need to specify the number of columns required, but the software will calculate the width of the columns, the page size and left- and right-margin requirements. (See Figure 2.1.6.)

Fonts

A **font**, or the **typeface** being used, is a design for the shape of the characters. Each font can be selected in a variety of **sizes**

and can also be used in any combination of bold, italic or underlined **styles**. These fonts can be selected either before or after the text has been typed in.

By changing the way the text looks in a document, you are able to:

- make important words and ideas prominent
- make the meaning of words and paragraphs clearer
- make more text fit onto a page.

Printers also have a range of fonts, font sizes and font styles, and some have colours as well. (See Figure 2.1.7.)

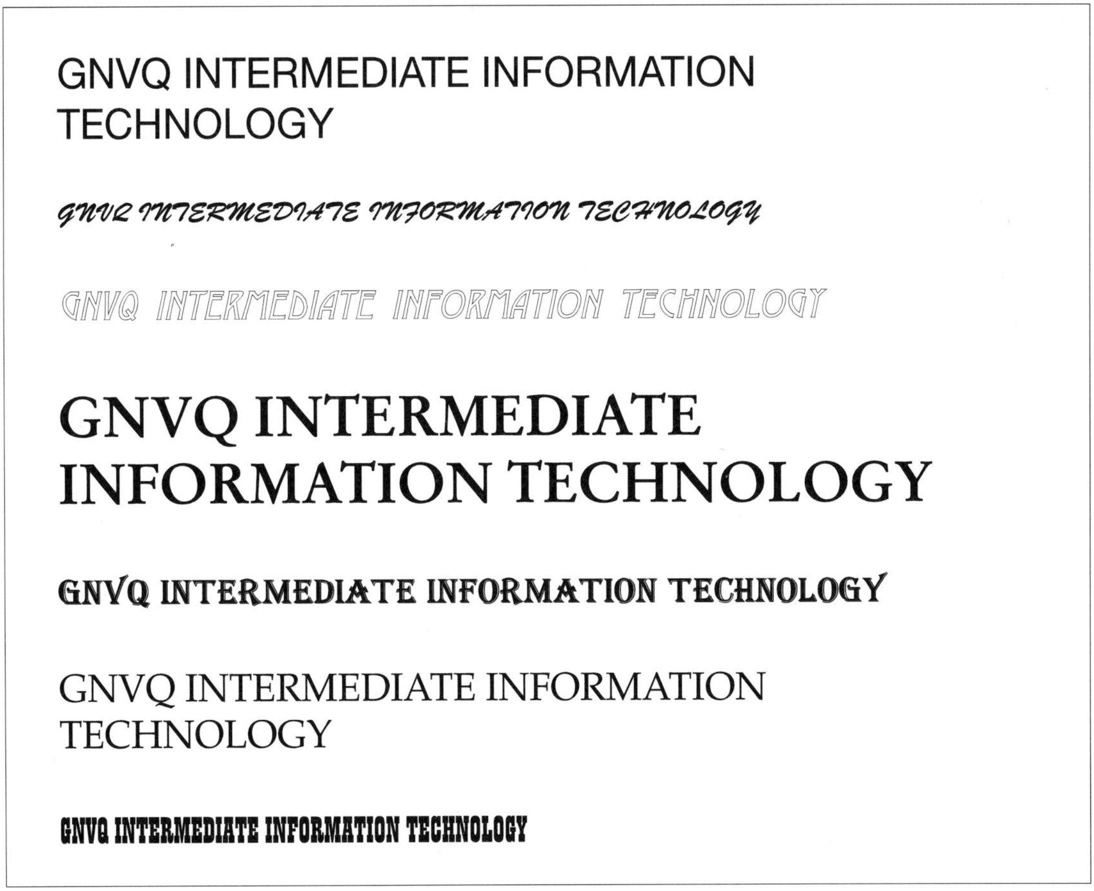

GNVQ INTERMEDIATE INFORMATION TECHNOLOGY

GNVQ INTERMEDIATE INFORMATION TECHNOLOGY

GNVQ INTERMEDIATE INFORMATION TECHNOLOGY

GNVQ INTERMEDIATE INFORMATION TECHNOLOGY

GNVQ INTERMEDIATE INFORMATION TECHNOLOGY

GNVQ INTERMEDIATE INFORMATION TECHNOLOGY

GNVQ INTERMEDIATE INFORMATION TECHNOLOGY

FIGURE 2.1.7 *Seven different types and sizes of font*

Footers and headers

There may be occasions when you require additional information to be included on each page of a document. This information could include any or all of the following:

- page numbering
- chapter titles
- the date
- a word or words which must go on each page.

If any of this information is to be shown at the top margin of the document, then it is known as a **header**. Alternatively, if it is to appear at the foot of each page, then it is a **footer**. If these headers or footers are not required on each page, then it is possible to **suppress** their printing on some pages.

Headers and footers can have more than one line and can include items such as drawings or objects. Once they have been inserted in a document, all other functions remain as normal, and they do not affect any of the remaining formatting jobs you might want to do.

Indents

Indents control the space between the page margins and the paragraphs. Setting a larger left indent increases the blank space to the left of a paragraph. The use of indents helps to make the following easier to read:

- bulleted or numbered points
- separate paragraphs, even if the first line only is indented
- quotations
- important items which need to be made clearer to the reader.

Justification

Justification refers to the right-hand margin of a document. A **justified** right margin means that each line of the text

finishes at exactly the same point, giving a straight margin the same as the left one. Because this does not happen naturally, the computer and printer will adjust the spacing along the whole line of text to ensure that the last letters always finish in the same place. This gives slightly irregular spacing along the line, but does give a very professional-looking document once it is printed. An unjustified right margin is also known as a **ragged** right margin since each lines ends at a different place.

Line spacing

All documents created from new will be in **single line spacing**. It is possible, however, to very simply and automatically change this to a different required line spacing. There may be some times when printing a section in **double line spacing** instead would make it easier to read and would emphasise its importance within the document. If this section were in the middle of the page, it would be possible to change to double line spacing at the beginning of it and then reselect single line spacing after it. If the document is particularly long and likely to be read in great detail, then it is always wisest to print in double line spacing to make it less tiring for the reader to scan.

Margins

Page and **margin** settings determine how the work will look when printed on a hard copy. You can select the command to change the margin settings of a document, and this determines the distance between the text and the edges of the paper. You can change the margins to make room for the following reasons:

- to make room for headers and footers
- to leave space for a personal or company letterhead paper
- to change the number of pages in the document

- to leave room for the document to be bound together
- to improve the look or readability of the document.

Once the margins have been changed, they will remain the same throughout the document until you select them to be altered.

Page numbering

As we have already mentioned, **page numbering** can be inserted as a footer. Alternatively, a 'page numbering' option can be selected separately. This facility allows the page number to be inserted at a choice of locations, e.g., bottom centre or bottom right, and also enables the user to choose the page at which numbering will commence – you may not wish the first page to be numbered, or you may wish the first page to be, say, number five.

Tabulations

When text or numerical information is arranged side-by-side on a page in a document, it is easier to read and more understandable. Whilst a table can be created using the 'Tab' key, an easier and much quicker way is to create a table in a spreadsheet and import it into the word-processed document. Obviously, this is only possible if you are using an integrated software package. Tabulation itself in word-processing software, however, can easily be mastered once the setting and deletion of tab stops has been managed.

If the tabulation is a simple one, then the information should be keyed in across the columns, line by line, using the tab key to get from one column to another. If, however, the tabulation is more complicated and lines are required around the table and between the columns, then this can be achieved in a quite easy way either by selecting the 'line draw' facility or by creating a table template and keying the text into the pre-formed boxes.

2.1.3 Enter data and edit the document

Data

In this performance criteria, you must show your competence at entering different types of data into a software application and then prove that you can retrieve that document and edit it in a variety of different ways. To help you to gain evidence here, we have provided some simple activities for you to complete and print out for inclusion in your portfolio of evidence.

Graphics: copy, move, rotate, size

You now need to practise and show that you can carry out all of the above range statements competently. Complete the activity on page 55 and print out a copy for your tutor to assess. This can then be included in your portfolio of evidence.

GNVQ INTERMEDIATE INFORMATION TECHNOLOGY

The term 'database' relates to what can be called an electronic filing system. In fact, most accounting software and spreadsheets are specialised databases. Most organisations would use and maintain a database in one form or another in order to:

> collect and store information regarding customers or clients

> to profile products sold or purchased

> to collect and store personnel records.

A database is a collection of records. Each record is structured into fields and each field contains specific information. The desired structure and range of records can be flexible and can be compiled by the operator and, as such, is a formal way of storing information. The record would be a collection of facts about a specific product, client or supplier. It could also hold a list of records regarding stock, prices and number of units sold.

Before embarking on the installation of a database system, the organisation would need to ensure that the package would be suitable. In addition, it would need to decide whether a general package would suffice or whether one more closely related to the activities of the business were required.

64   STUDENT INFORMATION

FIGURE 2.1.8 *An example of a document page which has incorporated a header, a footer, page numbering, single and double spacing, an indent and a justified right margin*

student activity

● **IT** 2.1, 2.2, 2.3 CLAIT (OPTION) IBT2

Start up your application software that will permit you to produce a graphic image of the following set of data:

BOOK TITLE	% OF MARKET
Information Technology	37.8
More IT	23.5
Want to Learn IT?	12.5
Worried About IT?	12.0
Be an Expert in IT	14.2

1 Save your data.
2 Create a bar chart (including labels), and enter the heading 'UK BOOK MARKET'.
3 Save your chart, and print one copy.

Tables: delete (row, column, data), insert (row, column, data), size (row, column)

You now need to practise and show that you can carry out all of the above range statement competently. Complete the next activity and print out a copy for your tutor to assess. This can then be included in your portfolio of evidence.

student activity

● **IT** 2.1, 2.2, 2.3, CLAIT IBT2

Start up your spreadsheet software.

1 Enter the title 'EXPENSES CLAIMS'.
2 On the row below the title, enter the following column headings:

   NAME PETROL ENTERTAINMENT SUNDRIES TOTAL

   You should widen your columns to allow each title to be accommodated.
3 Now you should enter the following data:

   ● Names: Brian Forbes, Colin Cruickshank, Patricia Barnes, Harry Murgatroyd, Joseph Harris
   ● Brian Forbes is claiming the following expenses: Petrol £75, Entertainment £117, Sundries £17.50
   ● Colin Cruickshank is claiming the following expenses: Petrol £87.50, Entertainment £50.75, Sundries £5.60
   ● Patricia Barnes is claiming the following expenses: Petrol £15.55, Entertainment £67.50, Sundries £11.75
   ● Harry Murgatroyd is claiming the following expenses: Petrol £95.00, Entertainment £50.75, Sundries £10.25
   ● Joseph Harris is claiming the following expenses: Petrol £18.00, Entertainment £86.99, Sundries £13.00.

4 Enter suitable formulae to calculate the TOTAL column.
5 Print a copy of your spreadsheet.
6 Now make the following changes:

- Harry Murgatroyd has already claimed these particular expenses, so his records can be deleted from the claims sheet.
- Joseph Harris has made an error in his claim, and it should read £66.99

and not £86.99 – please amend
- Pamela Chaston had forgotten to submit her claim form. Please add the following: Petrol £16.75, Entertainment £44.60, Sundries £5.00; and calculate her total expense claim.

7 Save and print a copy of your amended spreadsheet.

Text: copy, delete, enhance, insert, move

You now need to practise and show that you can carry out all of the above range statements competently. Complete the next activity and print out a copy for your tutor to assess. This can then be included in your portfolio of evidence.

student activity

● **IT** 21,. 2.2, 2.3, CLAIT IBT2

Start up your word-processing software and open a new file. Enter the following text:

ONE OF THE JOYS OF FRANCE

The Loire Valley was so named after the long river that wound its way through it. People from all over the world used to travel to this fabled land. Men of power flocked to Tours, Bloise and Orleans and turned them into the area's intellectual and political centres. Men of religion came to towns like Bourges and Chartres to build the immense Gothic cathedrals. Men of words came to admire the Loire Valley's legendary beauty.

Today, the Loire Valley's story continues, with people coming to sample gastronomic as well as visual delights, and some of France's best known wines are produced here.

Grapes ripen well in this mild climate, as do pears, strawberries and cherries.

It is not surprising, therefore, that the Loire Valley temps so many tourists each year, and that those tourists enjoy exploring, cycling, playing golf, horseriding or visiting some of the many chateaux, as well as sampling the fine wines!

Save your text and print out one copy. Retrieve your file onto the screen and make the following changes:

1 Delete the sentence 'People from all over the world used to travel to this fabled land.'

2 Move the paragraph beginning 'Grapes ripen well in this ... ' so that it becomes the final sentence of the first paragraph.

3 Centre and embolden the heading.

4 Insert, as a final paragraph, the following:
    It is understandable then that France has become so popular. After all, this is only

and then copy the emboldened heading so that it completes this final paragraph.

Save your work, and print out one copy.

2.1.4 Find and combine data from given sources

Find: by looking in the right directory; by looking for files with a given name

For this performance criteria, you will need to be observed by your tutor. He/she will give you file names which you will have to find, either from a different directory or by their title, and then retrieve. It may be that your tutor will have a checklist which they complete whilst you are carrying out this straightforward task, or you may be given a log which you complete each time you successfully complete an activity of this kind. Whichever method of recording this assessment is used, it is important that you file this away in your portfolio so that you can prove competence on more than one occasion for the external verifier when he/she visits your school or college.

2.1.5 Save using appropriate file names and apply accuracy and security checks

File names

As we have mentioned previously, it is possible to call a document or file anything that you choose. There are, however, some restrictions, and these include the fact that a file name cannot have more than eight characters. Obviously, it is important not only that you call the file something appropriate that you can easily and readily identify the next time you want to retrieve it, but also that anybody else who has access to your files can understand the system of naming that you use. (e.g. when you are on leave from work)

Accuracy checks

It is important, not only for the purposes of this course but also for any work situation, that documents or material you produce be accurate. There are several methods that can be used to check work for accuracy, and each are covered under the range statements given below. Accurate work will be required of you once you commence employment, whether it be text or numerical data that you are handling, so it is best to get into good habits about checking for accuracy whilst you are still learning.

Proofreading

Proofreading means reading the screen for errors before you print out your work, and also then checking the hard copy to ensure that you have not missed anything on screen. It is much easier to proofread the hard copy because, for some reason, we all seem to miss mistakes when they are on the screen. In order to assist you in practising this skill, we have given you the following activity to carry out:

student activity

● **COM** 1.2

The following text contains 14 errors. Can you find them all?

Once upon a time, chopping was a labor. Sleeves were rolled up, ther was huffing and puffing, as the cook set to weilding a cleever to reduce the size of a large joint of meet. She would pound sugar or spices to a powder with a pestle and morter, and rub fruits through a clothe to make a puree.

It is little wonder that labour-saving devises were greeted so enthusisticly. Some were wierd, some practicle, but they mostly helped to lighten the load of the cooks who used them.

Now we have electric servents, with blades to chop, grind and great, and I, for one, appreciate them, but we must be careful that this doesn't make for boring meals.

Proofreading is described as the visual checking of documents to ensure that the content and layout of text and the positioning of tables and graphics is correct. The British Standards Institute has produced guidelines in its BS5261 of symbols which can be used for proof-reading purposes.

student activity

● **COM** 2.1
● **IT** 2.1, 2.2, 2.3

In pairs, consult your school or college library and research the content of the BS5261 mentioned above. Summarise the content in the form of a word-processed report for your tutor, and include the symbols that the British Standards Institute recommends.

Spellcheck

Many word-processing programs have a **spellchecking** facility. This means that the computer will scan the document, file or page for inaccuracies in spelling. The accessing of this facility varies from program to program, but usually the cursor needs to be at the top of the screen and then the instruction is given. The cursor will highlight any word that the computer does not recognise and will allow you either to choose the correct option from the list of options, or to edit the word. It is also possible, when spellchecking, to add words to the dictionary in the memory of the computer for future use.

(For more on accuracy checks, see Element 3.4, pages 117–120.)

Security checks

When saving work on a computer file, it is important to remember that you may not want anybody else to access this information, particularly if it is of a confidential nature. Most organisations that use a network system will have certain security processes which their employees will have to carry out when using the computers. These processes may include **log-in** and **log-out** procedures, as well as the use of **code words** or **passwords** for accessing certain levels of information. In other words, very junior members of staff will have passwords which allow them to access only certain files, whereas more senior staff or management will have passwords which allow them compete access to all files.

Naturally, it is always wise to make a **back-up copy** of any information saved. This can be done by saving both on hard drive and on floppy disk, or by disk-copying the floppy disk so that two copies are available.

Copyright on data and software

There are certain restrictions laid down by legislation as to the work produced by another individual or organisation that can be copied without breaching **copyright**

legislation. The copyright symbol (as mentioned in the activity below) indicates when this legislation has to be adhered to.

student activity

Using your college or school library, research the legislation relating to the copyright of documents. What does the copyright symbol look like? Present your findings in the form of a short report for the attention of your tutor. Ensure that you cover the main points of the legislation and the restrictions as far as reproducing in any form are concerned.

Regular saving

Whenever you are using a computer, whether it be for word processing, spreadsheets, a database or graphic design, it is important to 'save as you go' rather than waiting until the task has been completed. Several problems could arise which you have no control over – e.g. a power cut – which could mean that you lose your work. By saving regularly throughout the task, you will at least have kept the work completed and not left yourself open to a great deal of extra work and frustration.

Theft of equipment or software

It is always wise to be aware at all times of the risk of theft of any kind. It is particularly important, however, to ensure that the equipment you use is protected at all times from the risk of theft. In addition, the software being used should always be kept safe, particularly if it is backed up on floppy disk, as it is much more tempting for a thief to take a set of disks than it is to remove the whole computer system from a room!

Keep the source document

Having completed your piece of work, it is sensible to retain the original **source document** for future reference. It may be that the piece of work was for another employee of the organisation, and that they may wish to make changes to it.

Alternatively, an error could be found which may be blamed on your inputting skills, in which case if you have the original document, you will be able to identify when the error was made.

(For more on security matters, see Element 3.4.)

2.1.6 Produce documents and suggest improvements

In this performance criteria, you have to show that you are capable of producing documents. You will be carrying out this task throughout the study of this performance criteria, and you will provide the required evidence in the end-of-element assignment. During the course of this activity or series of activities, you will be asked to make some improvements. These improvements will include:

- **improvements to the specification**
- **improvements to your own documents**
- **improvements to other documents.**

It is important that you show you are competent in each of these tasks, and that you retain the evidence for inclusion in your portfolio.

This element is a very practical one in nature, and it could be used to create a report for another element from the specification. It could be integrated with Element 3.1 which looks both at different information flowing throughout an organisation and at the data-processing systems it uses. Alternatively, it could be linked to Element 1.1. which looks at industrial and commercial systems in general.

Your teacher/tutor will provide you with a list of descriptions of a range of documents which you have to produce, and you will be able to choose ideas for

their presentation and layout, using suitable software. These documents may be produced using any of the software we have already mentioned in this element and in Unit 1.

Your evidence will be a report or a written account which clearly states what were your observed activities, when and where they took place, who was involved and why you carried them out. Remember that it is very important that you are observed several times, and that you obtain written evidence for inclusion in your portfolio.

2.2

Process graphic designs

2.2.1

Identify types of graphic design software and give examples

The amount of **graphic design software** available to organisations and to individuals is growing rapidly. Such software packages include PowerPoint, CorelDraw and Claris' Impact which all allow the user to produce high-quality graphics material. We intend in this performance criteria to look briefly at the different kinds of graphic image.

Bitmap

Bitmap graphics are a graphic image or text formed by a pattern or dots or **pixels**. An **electronic graphic file** stores each minute item (known as a dot) in a graphic picture. These items are represented by a single (or several for colour) **bit** of information in the file. A picture which contains 8,000 bits of information will produce a 1,000-byte file as 1 byte is equal to 8 bits. One of the drawbacks with bitmap graphics is that they cannot be scaled in the way that vector-based images can.

Vector

Vector graphics are graphic images where the graphic elements are defined by using **coordinate geometry**. This enables them to be scaled up or down without any loss of resolution. Each of the lines or circles in a vector graphic can be manipulated or moved about individually.

Chart

It is said that information presented in a

chart format is easier to understand and to explain than any other method of communication. When we talk about the term chart, we include **pie charts**, **histograms**, **line graphs**, **scatter graphs** and pictures. With the use of a scanner, it is possible to include a picture, image or diagram in any presentation being prepared, or to choose a picture from a range of **clip art** held in the software being used.

Slide-show presentations

Software such as the Microsoft PowerPoint allows the user to create a series of graphic images which can be produced as **slides**, and the **slide sequence** can be rearranged to suit the user. When the user has created the slides to their own satisfaction, the computer can be used to project the various images onto a monitor or a large screen. Each of the individual slides will be projected for a specified period of time, or alternatively, the manual operation can be selected which allows the user to determine when the next slide is shown.

2.2.2 Identify the graphic components required to meet given design specifications

Graphic components

In this performance criteria, we look at the various components which make up the graphic image produced by software. Graphic images, as we already know, are made up of a combination of lines and shapes, and this allows the competent user to produce an image of their choice. When we have considered these graphic components, we shall discuss the considerations needed when meeting a design specification.

Attributes

Each graphic image produced can be amended to change the thickness of the line (or of the border around the image) and the colour or depth of either the **filled** section or the shadow being used. These attributes allow the user to highlight particular areas or to make the image more definite for use on a projector screen.

Brush

In much the same way as an artist would brush paint onto a canvas, it is possible to achieve the same effect by using the mouse on the screen. Different thicknesses of brush and various colour options can be selected and 'painted' onto the screen. Errors can then be erased using the 'erase' tool.

Colour

The use of colour for a presentation will obviously enhance the impact on the audience, and it is possible to use colour with most software available. Bold colours tend to be most effective, as paler shades tend not to be so noticeable when projected. The use of colour may be quite effective, but it is very expensive and therefore tends not to be used.

Lines and shapes

We have already mentioned the facility which allows the user to select the different width of line, but it is also possible to choose the style of line being used. The most commonly used line styles are:

- straight
- arc
- curve
- freehand.

From these four line styles, it is possible to create almost any shape.

However, it would not be feasible or cost-effective to have to make every shape the user requires. For this reason, there are also a series of shapes available for selection, and these include:

- circles
- polygons
- rectangles.

Spray

In much the same way as the user can 'brush' paint onto the screen, 'spraying' can also be used. This gives the effect of an aerosol spray, and the result can be quite impressive. Most packages allow the selection of various sprays, including stars, snow and dots.

Text

For most word-processed documents, the normal size of the print is either 10 or 12 pitch. This, however, is not always suitable for graphic-design use or for slide-show presentations, as these do not project particularly well; nor do they always emphasise important pieces of information. Most software packages which are designed for use with graphics or presentations allow the user to consider these display requirements, and they often have a pre-set text size which

accommodates all the considerations. Often, the most suitable method of displaying text for presentations is by using bold headings and bullet points, with a smaller text beside each point. It is advisable not to cram too much information onto one slide but to use key points on a number of them.

Design specifications

This section deals with the design specification which will be given to you as part of an assignment. You will have to consider the key points, and we list the key areas needing consideration under the following range statements.

Purpose

The first place to start is to think about *why* the design specification has been given to you. You will be spending a lot of time and effort in preparing this graphic design or presentation material, and you need to know from the outset the purpose of this effort. You will also need to confirm how many copies will be needed in the future. Is this just a one-off presentation, or will many more copies be needed over a long period of time?

What, furthermore, is the level of ability of the person you are doing the work for? Do they have any technical knowledge, or do you need to make the detail very plain and straightforward?

Content and dimensions

Having identified the purpose of the design, it will also be necessary to consider the content. You will have to think about the best way to portray the information to the audience. Does the content have to be drawn to scale? Will the content require a series of sub-drawings in order to explain some detail? Will all of the information fit onto one drawing, or will this be confusing and be best spread over a series of drawings?

Dimensions will include the size of a single element or component in the measurement units used.

Tolerance refers to the maximum errors in size that a manufactured article may have and that are indicated on a production drawing.

Graphic type

We have already discussed the bitmap and vector graphics, as well as the possibility of producing charts or slides to present information. You will have to consider which method you can use to the best effect.

If you need to draw such items as **organisational charts** or **flow charts**, then vector graphics are often used. This is known as **block schematics**.

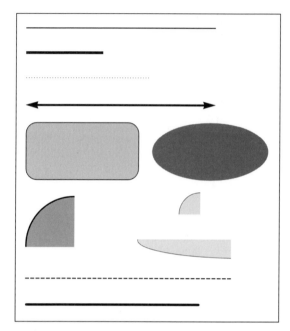

FIGURE 2.2.1 *Different line styles, thickness and shading facilities*

Set the image and page attributes

This is very obviously a practical performance criteria, and you are now required to set the image and page attributes for a piece of work you have been given to design. We refresh your memory on the requirements of the range statements below.

Image attributes

Image attributes include thickness of line and the type of line used, both of which will obviously determine the way your image looks. They also include the following:

Colours

Remember that colour can be very impressive, but be careful not to use pastel shades as these do not show up too well. Also be aware again of the *cost* of producing work using colour.

Height and width

You will need to be aware of the final printed height of your graphics. As we see in this section, it is possible to change the top and bottom and the left- and right-hand margins so that you have the maximum amount of paper to use. It is also possible to 'stretch' the size of clip-art drawings to make them taller, shorter,

FIGURE 2.3.1 *The cockpit of a flight simulator, seen here approaching Hong Kong airport at dusk*

staff than it would if it had carried out the real change of procedure or process itself. Additionally, it is also less dangerous in some circumstances to carry out modelling than the real event, particularly if the latter involves the use of toxic or hazardous chemicals.

Models are usually easy to set up and to run, particularly if the testing or modelling involves several re-runs under different circumstances, e.g. with different temperatures or noise levels.

Because computer models can be built to represent almost identically the 'real thing' and to react to circumstances and situations in a similar way, this kind of modelling is often known as **simulation**. Good examples of simulation include pilot-training and car-driving situations where the user is put into the driver's position in a plane or car and given a series of different situations to deal with.

Prediction and gaming

Predictive models enable the user to forecast possible future events. Typically, spreadsheet models here allow you to forecast break-even points or financial information or produce graphs of mathematical functions, as well as predict profits. Another method of operating prediction models involves different business games played by team members who set a series of business strategies. The computer will take the strategies given by the different team members, eliminate those with bad ideas and give varying grades to those with the best ideas. There are a wide variety of **game models** available, including car-driving games or complex adventure games which require a series of decisions to be made. Most of these games allow the rules to be changed, and the models then demonstrate the results of such changes.

student activity

● **COM** 2.1, 2.2

In pairs, ignoring the examples given above for prediction and gaming, to what other uses do you think these forms of modelling could realistically be put? Consider your ideas and then write a short memo giving your suggestions to your tutor.

Identify the data in a given numerical processing activity

Define the calculations required to produce a model of the activity

2.3.4

Construct a layout of a model and enter data

We have put all of these performance criteria together because essentially, in order to construct a model you will need to be including all three at the same time. When constructing a model of a given numerical processing activity, you look at three main elements:

1 *the data* – this is the information that the model will manipulate
2 *the calculations* – this is the way the model is constructed in order to manipulate the data
3 *the layout* – this is the way the model will be presented.

The first place to start is to plan or design a rough model – known as a **blueprint**. This will help you to foresee any possible problems or difficulties and to identify all the data needed for the construction of the model itself.

Let us now consider the above three main elements in turn:

Identifying the data

In order to create a model, you need four different types of data: **number**, **date**,

character and **formula** (we shall look at formulae under the next heading). The numbers and characters can be entered in the font styles and sizes required. When using a spreadsheet program, the following characters are termed numbers – anything else from the keyboard is termed as text:

$$0\ 1\ 2\ 3\ 4\ 5\ 6\ 7\ 8\ 9 + n - / \pounds\ \%$$

Numbers can also be termed **constants** because in a spreadsheet program they are not entered after an '=' sign.

When entering numbers as dates, it is important to format the date column when setting up the model. If this task is not carried out and the date (or the time) is entered using the division sign (/) – e.g. '25 January' entered as '25/01', – then the spreadsheet program will treat this as a fraction and will carry out a calculation instead.

As we mentioned earlier, characters (or text) other than numbers are usually entered into a spreadsheet program in order to describe an item or items. Text must be kept separate from numbers: the program will not be able to make number calculations if a combination of numbers and text is entered into one column.

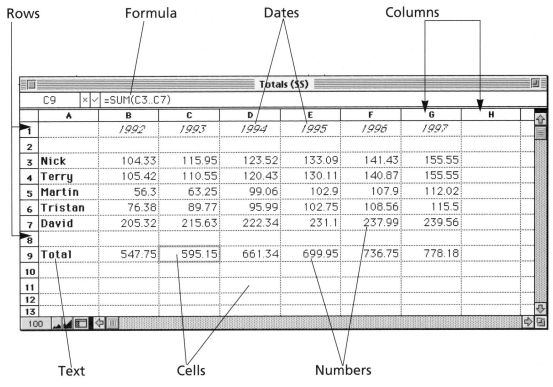

FIGURE 2.3.2 *An example of a spreadsheet layout*

Defining the calculations

In order to make a calculation using a spreadsheet program, it is necessary for you to enter a **formula**. Formulae allow you to make a variety of different calculations 'automatically', which means that the computer will react instantaneously. Obviously, when you designed your blueprint, you decided what type of calculation you had to make to construct the model (this is known as the **manual calculation**).

The following character signs on the keyboard are important when entering formulae:

= is always entered before the formula
+ is entered when two **cells** are being added together

– is entered when one cell is being subtracted from another
/ is entered when one cell is being divided by another
* is entered when one cell is being multiplied by another

When entering a formula, the correct cell should be highlighted, and then the '=' sign goes in first, followed by the required information. For example:

'=C5+C6' requires that cell C5 be added to cell C6

'=C7–C2' requests that cell C2 be subtracted from cell C7.

It is a good idea to make sure that you understand this section regarding formulae, as it is possible to make very simple calculations using them and also to progress onto much more complicated ones, still using the same symbols shown above. For example:

'=sum(B1:B9)' requests that the whole of **row** B be added together to give the total. The ':' represents the words 'through to'

'=B4*2.5 %' requests that cell B4 be multiplied by 2.5 per cent to calculate the percentage discount a customer is entitled to.

All of the symbols we have discussed so far are known as **arithmetic operators** because they perform basic calculations such as adding, subtracting, dividing and multiplying. However, there are also other operators, known as **relational operators** or **comparison operators**, which include the following:

= represents equal to
> represents greater than
< represents less than.

We shall look in more detail at these comparison operators in Element 3.3 of this book.

Constructing the layout

There are three main areas to consider when deciding on the layout of your model, to ensure that it is presented clearly: the **row**, **column** and **cell** formats. Most programs will allow you easily to adjust the height of each row as well as the width of the columns. This is usually done by placing the cursor on the dividing line at the top of each column division and moving the mouse until a broken cross appears. It is then possible to 'drag' the mouse until the desired width of column is obtained. As an alternative, you can choose the 'column width' or 'row height' options from the 'format' option on the menu.

It is also possible to change the style and size of font when using spreadsheet programs. This is done in much the same way as when using a word-processing program, although you have the added benefit of being able to highlight one or more particular cells as required.

The number types used can involve a number of formats:

- use of a number of decimal places
- use of the 'per cent' sign
- use of the '£' or the '$' sign for currencies
- use of the ',' sign to separate thousands
- use of scientific symbols
- use of brackets around numbers. In accounting terms, this represents a minus figure, although the alternative is to represent with a minus sign or in red.

Undertake 'What if' queries for the model

2.3.6 Save the file, back up regularly and produce the required output

The exact nature of a 'what if' query will obviously depend on the processing activities being resolved. In an organisation, a 'what if' query could typically be used to find out the effect on production costs if the quality of goods produced is increased. Other examples include working out break-even points so that an organisation can assess how many units need to be sold at a particular price in order to recover its costs.

Obviously, when constructing your model, you will need to carry out some 'what if' calculations. Remember that whenever you make these calculations, you should produce evidence so that you can prove your competence in this activity.

Similarly, you should also ensure that you prove your competence at saving, backing up and printing at various stages of your element assignment to obtain evidence for performance criteria 2.3.6.

It is possible that you have had the opportunity to integrate this element with Element 2.4 which deals with process control systems. Alternatively, you may have progressed through some of the learning stages by using the tutorial sections of some software applications, particularly database and control software.

task 1

Produce a record which shows that you have identified different types of model. Give one example of each.

task 2

Show that you have identified at least two types of data in a given numerical processing activity.

task 3

Produce a record which shows that you have defined at least three types of calculation.

task 4

Construct the layout of the model and enter the required data.

task 5

Produce a record which shows that you have undertaken at least two 'what if' queries.

task 6

Produce a record which shows that you have saved and backed up files regularly and produced the required output.

element

Use information technology for process control

Describe the uses of process control systems

In this element of Unit 2, we need to look in some detail at the different ways an organisation can use technology to control various areas of its activity. The different **process control systems** that we discuss throughout this section of the book are very important throughout different parts of industry, as well as to us as individuals. Without process control systems, life would be very unpleasant! For instance, such systems make our lives more comfortable by:

- controlling the temperature of our everyday environment by the use of thermostats for central heating systems
- keeping our environment safe by the use of smoke alarms
- making our roads safe by the use of traffic lights
- making our journeys safe by the use of street lighting
- ensuring our clothes are cleaned

properly by the use of washing machines
- ensuring our food is cooked safely by the use of thermostats and timers on our cookers.

Process control systems are used for the following reasons, and we look at each through the relevant range statements:

- environmental control
- process production control
- quality control
- control of security.

Let us consider each of these in turn.

Environmental control

Environmental control systems do as the name implies: they control our everyday environment. For instance, our central heating systems control air and water temperatures in order that we can relax, shower or bathe in a comfortable home environment. Similarly, in our schools or colleges, the central heating system is controlling the working environment for all of us. Obviously, it is important that the fuel which is used to heat and then circulate the hot water by means of a pump around the radiators in our heating system be controlled effectively so that the temperature does not continue to rise and rise. This heat-control mechanism is known as a **thermostat**, and when the temperature reaches the value set on the thermostat, the fuel supply is closed down so that less heat is given off. Naturally, once the room has cooled down enough, the thermostat will 'click in' again and allow the fuel to heat some more water to pump around the radiators.

student activity

● **COM** 2.1, 2.2

Can you think of any other environmental-control systems which we use in our everyday life? Write a list of all those that come to mind, and then compare your list to those of the rest of your group.

Process production control

For organisations involved in manufacturing products, it is very important that they carry out effective and efficient control procedures to ensure that they are both producing goods of a high quality and doing so in the most cost-effective and labour-saving way.

We looked at computer-aided manufacture (CAM) in Element 1.1 of this book, and the use of the **microprocessors** for this purpose is carried through to the production process. Microprocessors have become increasingly important in process production control for two main reasons: their ability to be programmed; and their ability to connect to other systems. Before the introduction of microprocessors, all such processes were controlled manually or mechanically.

When a CAM designer uses software to design a machine, we already know that he/she 'draws' the whole machine or parts of the machine on a computer screen, possibly by using a light-pen. While this process is taking place, the computer is producing a magnetic tape which will eventually control the way the machine operates. This facility enables the designer to make very specific process-control decisions and to give detailed instructions about the production process itself. Microprocessor-based control systems have enabled organisations to become more profitable as well as more efficient and effective, because they allow a more immediate response to changes.

Process production control systems will be found in the following industries:

● chemicals
● steel and aluminium
● food and beverages
● petroleum products.

Quality control

In consultation with the sales department, the production department of an organisation must make sure that it can supply customers with the quantity required at the time they have been requested. The tight monitoring of production levels means that the production department should know how long it would take to produce enough products to meet a particular order. Advanced planning and close liaison with the sales department is vital here.

Regardless of how many units of products are being produced, the production department is also responsible for the maintenance of quality. Each product must meet a number of strict quality standards, and must to all intents and purposes be exactly the same every time. Periodically, products will be randomly selected from the production line and tested by either the research and development (R&D) department or the quality-assurance-control department. A good production department will monitor methods of production used by all major competitors and allied industries and take steps to implement any useful methods of production used elsewhere. Increasingly, as production becomes steadily more automated, the production department will also have to either design computer programs or 'buy in' computer programs which can handle the new processes.

The use of information technology in quality control has increased in recent years, and more and more industries are using IT to ensure that their products are of the highest possible quality. This is particularly true of industries that produce goods of various different qualities.

Control of security

Technological advances over recent years have made it much easier for individuals and organisations to make their premises more secure. At home, we use a variety of different security systems to ensure that we are safe. These include:

- intruder alarms
- timers which can be set to switch on radios and lights at various times during the day and evening

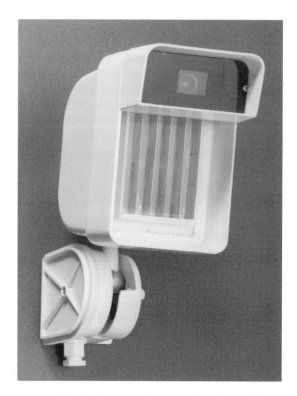

FIGURE 2.4.1 *An example of a movement-sensitive camera detector*

- movement- or heat-sensitive cameras which switch on automatically when the house is approached.

These security systems all include the use of **sensors** which monitor our environment and switch on either when a change takes place or when they have been pre-set to do so. The types of sensor which are used in security systems are:

- light
- heat
- movement
- infra-red
- sound
- pressure pads.

Organisations also use these security systems on their buildings or warehouses to ensure that unwanted visitors are detected at the earliest stage possible so that assistance can be sought. Very often, their security-control systems are connected directly to the emergency services so that the police, for example, are notified instantly of any security threat or situation.

2.4.2 Identify stages in a given process control system

In any process control system, three crucial stages will be involved. We shall now look at these three different stages, using the heating of a kiln for the firing of pottery as our example.

1 *Sense the conditions.* Obviously, for the successful firing of pottery in a kiln, the temperature has to be kept at a constant temperature. The process control system used in the production and manufacture of such pottery will need to 'sense' that the temperature is remaining constant and to detect immediately any changes that may be taking place.
2 *Compare the conditions with pre-set limits.* The sensor used to monitor the temperature of the kiln will have been given pre-set limits, e.g. not to reach a temperature above a certain level, or not to allow the temperature to fall below a certain level. The pre-set limits given in the case of the temperature of the kiln will involve a minimum and a maximum temperature, and anything below or above these temperatures will not be acceptable to the process control system.
3 *Adjust the output if necessary.* If the temperature of the kiln does not reach the minimum level, then the sensor will be activated and the heating process will be increased. If the temperature of the kiln goes above the maximum level, then the sensor will be activated and the kiln allowed to cool down until it reaches the correct temperature.

These three stages in the process control system are also known as a **loop**. They give feedback to the designer of the control system so that he/she can make adjustments and reprogramme.

Other stages in process control systems allow machinery to increase or decrease the speed at which they work. Alternatively, the machines can have pre-set limits which determine when they are switched on or off and which measure or count the output.

2.4.3 Describe the components of process control systems

Select and use components to construct a control system to a given specification

Review the performance of the control system and suggest improvements to the specification

Components

In this performance criteria, we will be investigating the different components which make up a process control system. Your teacher/tutor will provide you with an example of a process control system for you to use, and from this and the information given below you should be able to identify the stages within it. You are required to construct a control system from a given specification and then to review its performance and suggest any improvements to the specification.

Sensors

We have already discussed the use of sensors to detect different elements and the nearness of individuals to equipment or premises, as used in intruder alarms and fire alarms.

Sensors are also available which are activated by contact. The keyboard on a computer, for example, uses a contact sensor in the form of a **micro-switch** which is activated when the key is pressed, with a signal then sent to the processor.

Light and proximity sensors, in addition to being used in intruder alarms and timed security systems, are also found in the automatic focus facility on cameras and camcorders. An infra-red light beam monitors the distance between the camera and the subject of the photograph and sets the focus to obtain the best picture. In a similar way, if there is not enough natural daylight for the camera to produce a satisfactory photograph, then the automatic flash will cut in to provide the additional light required. It is also possible for a camera to sense the speed of the film being used in the camera and to read the amount of photographs still available to be taken on the film. This is done by using an electronic code which is printed on the side of the film.

Processors

The examples we have given above which relate to the automatic flash and focus facilities on cameras and camcorders are examples of **processors**. These are common in most of our everyday activities, and they perform tasks in a variety of different situations and circumstances, e.g.:

- in computers – in the central processing unit
- in cars
- in washing machines
- in dishwashers.

Taking the dishwasher as an example here, the processor would perform the following tasks:

- accept the instructions to wash the dishes on the selected program
- select the correct temperature of water for that program
- measure the temperature of that water
- monitor the temperature of the water throughout the selected program.

Control procedure

The **control procedure** refers to the control program which makes decisions about when a sense input has reached its limit before taking some action to adjust the output. Traffic lights work using a control procedure via a control program. A light beam senses the number of cars which have passed and then changes the traffic-light sequence accordingly.

Output devices

In the traffic-lights example above, the traffic lights are the **output device**.

The type of output device employed will depend on what it is that the process control system is regulating. For example, water heaters are the output devices that regulate temperature, the speakers on a television regulate the volume of sound in the room, and traffic lights regulate the traffic flow.

student activity

● **COM** 2.1

Write a list of any other output devices you can think of.

student activity

● **COM** 2.1

Apart from the examples we have given of types of process control system, what others can you think of? Work in pairs and compare your suggestions to those of the rest of the group.

Interconnecting devices

The purpose of **interconnecting devices** is to connect the different components in a process control system. They do this by using **signals** and sensors to pass information to the processor. There are two types of signal:

1 *digital* – which are on/off signals, and tend to be used by computers.
2 *analogue* – which are continuous signals, e.g. sounds, and tend to be used by sensors.

The system must have an **input/output port** which connects the signals to the processor. This port will have an **analogue-to-digital converter** so that the analogue signals can be accepted and read by the digital processor. This will allow the processor to react to the signals and send a message back to the control system. The input/output port will translate the message from the processor to the control system using a digital-to-analogue converter. An example of this set-up is that of a burglar alarm which detects, through the sensor, an intruder, either by sound or by heat. The sensor sends the signal to the processor via the analogue-to-digital converter interconnecting device. The processor then informs the police via an alarm which itself is also activated by the digital-to-analogue interconnecting device.

The specification

In order to prove competence in this performance criteria, you are required to select and use components to construct a process control system to a given specification. This specification will be supplied to you by your teacher/tutor. In order to be successful in this task, you should consider the following points:

- what is the purpose of the system? Write yourself rough notes which list the reasons why the process control system is required
- what are the stages involved in the process control system? Draw yourself a rough diagram showing the different stages and listing the components required
- how will the stages be connected? Connect the stages and components on your diagram so that you can see how the specification fits.

You should now work through the range statements below to ensure that you have covered every aspect of the construction process before you make a start on the element assignment.

Process control limits

How is the process control system going to be used, and what are its limits? It is very difficult for us to give you any explicit advice or information here as it will very much depend on the type of process control system you design. A central heating system, as we saw, will have a minimum and maximum temperature that is acceptable, and those are its limits.

Purpose

The purpose of the process control system is your most important consideration. Without a full understanding of *why* the specification has been given to you, you will not be able to create or design a suitable process control system. Make sure that you fully understand the information that has been given to you, and ask your teacher/tutor if you have any reservations.

Response time

The term **response time** refers to the speed at which the process control system will read the signals and take action. This is particularly important when dealing with intruder or fire alarms, and for manufacturing control processes which are affected by extreme temperatures. In industrial situations, products may easily become ruined if the temperature is not constant, and as such, it is imperative that any changes in temperature be detected immediately. It is much easier to obtain a fast response time if the system being used is a simple one, and this should also be remembered when you are designing your system.

Sensors

We have discussed already, in some detail, the different types of sensor available and their different purposes. You will have to decide which sensor(s) will be most appropriate for the specification you have been given. You will also need to consider the type of feedback you require from the sensors.

Type of feedback

The type of feedback relates to the process where the output is fed back into the input. There are two different types of feedback:

1 *positive* – which results in increased output and could be the result of a temperature reaching only the minimum level and therefore needing to be increased
2 *negative* – which results in reduced

output and could be the result of a temperature reaching the maximum level and therefore needing to be reduced.

Having received feedback from the process control system, you must now review the progress you have made on this assignment and make constructive comments as to how you would improve the performance on a future occasion.

assignment

For the purposes of providing evidence for this performance criteria, you will have to prove that you have produced a control system with at least one sensor and one output device. In addition, you will need to provide computer outputs which show that you have selected and used components to construct a control system for a given specification provided by your teacher/tutor.

task 1

You must produce a report which describes the uses of process control systems.

task 2

You must include in your report a description of the stages involved in a process control system.

task 3

The next part of your report should describe the components of a control system.

task 4

For this task, you must produce the control system itself. You will be given a specification, and you will have to select and use components to construct your control system.

task 5

Having produced your control system, you must review its performance and suggest improvements to the specification.

End test questions

Questions 1 and 2 are related to Text 1.

Text 1

Corinna works as a secretary to the managing director. She is responsible for arranging the meetings of the Board on a regular basis.

1 Which of the following documents would Corinna issue to inform the Board of a forthcoming meeting?

   a a business letter
   b a memorandum
   c an invoice
   d an agenda.

2 Which of the following documents would Corinna issue to all those who attended the Board meeting detailing the items discussed and matters dealt with at the meeting?

   a an agenda
   b the minutes
   c a memorandum
   d a notice of meeting.

Questions 3 and 5 are related to Figure 1.

A→The term commercial documents simply relates to any pieces of paper which are in regular use within an organisation.

B→This can include the purchase, sales, payment and receipt of documents, but also documents such as letters, memos, invitations and notices. We intend to deal with some of these documents individually.

C→A business letter can be sent by an organisation to deal with many differing occurrences. Unlike a memorandum, a business letter will be sent outside the organisation.

FIGURE 1

3 Which ONE of the following has been used to produce the paragraph marked A?

   a single-line spacing
   b double-line spacing

82

c amended right margin

d amended left margin.

4 Which ONE of the following has been used to produce the paragraph marked B?

a single-line spacing

b double-line spacing

c amended right margin

d amended left margin.

5 Which ONE of the following has been used to produce the paragraph marked C?

a single-line spacing

b double-line spacing

c amended right margin

d amended left margin.

6 When word-processing a document, which TWO of the following would enhance the appearance of an important section?

1 emboldening

2 underlining

3 moving a paragraph

4 cutting a paragraph.

    a 1 and 2

    b 2 and 3

    c 3 and 4

    d 1 and 4.

7 Which of the following software options would you use to check the accuracy of a document which has been word-processed?

a edit

b copy

c spellcheck

d paste.

8 Why would an organisation use passwords for all users of their computers?

a to improve the quality of documents produced

b to maintain confidentiality

c to allow multi-users

d to ensure regular backup.

9 Why would an organisation use security tags on all major items of computer equipment?

a to maintain confidentiality

b to discourage theft

c to allow multi-users

d to ensure regular backup.

Question 10 is related to Figure 2.

10 What facility was used to insert the figure below into the text?

a file

b frame

c picture

d object.

FIGURE 2

Questions 11 to 14 are related to Figure 3.

A   PLEASE JOIN US FOR A

CELEBRATION

B

C   <u>KATIE IS GETTING MARRIED NEXT SATURDAY</u>

D   WE WANT TO WISH HER WELL

<u>COME ALONG TO THE LOCAL AT
LUNCH TIME ON FRIDAY</u>

FIGURE 3

11 Which of the following have been used in the invitation at section marked A?

   a   change font and embolden
   b   insert picture
   c   embolden
   d   underline.

12 Which of the following have been used in the invitation at section marked B?

   a   change font and embolden
   b   insert picture
   c   embolden
   d   underline.

13 Which of the following have been used in the invitation at section marked C?

   a   change font and embolden
   b   insert picture
   c   change font
   d   underline.

14 Which of the following have been used in the invitation at section marked D?

   a   change font and underline
   b   insert picture
   c   embolden
   d   underline.

15 When the instruction is given to print onto landscape paper, which of the following attributes are referred to?

   a   paper size
   b   image
   c   margins
   d   paper orientation

Questions 16 to 22 are related to Figure 4.

	A	B	C	D
1	ITEMS SOLD IN THE CURRENT YEAR			
2				
3	NAME	PRICE	QUANTITY	TOTAL PRICE
4				
5	CAMEO	12.99	5	64.95
6	BAISE	35.99	12	431.88
7	PHYLLIS	12.99	150	1948.5
8	DIANA	17.99	25	449.5
9				
10	TOTAL SALES			2894.83

FIGURE 4

16 Which of the following is shaded on the spreadsheet?

   a   a row
   b   a formula
   c   a title
   d   a column.

17 Which of the following formats has been used in cell A5?

   a   character
   b   scientific
   c   formula
   d   date.

18 Which of the following formats has been used in cell D5?

   a   character
   b   scientific
   c   formula
   d   date.

19 Which of the following formats has been used in cell D10?

   a   character
   b   scientific
   c   formula
   d   date.

20 Which of the following calculations has been made in cell D7?

   a   a relational calculation of B7 and C7?
   b   an addition of B7 and C7?
   c   a subtraction of B7 from C7?
   d   a multiplication of B7 and C7?

21 Which of the following calculations has been made in cell D10?

   a   a relational calculation of D5 to D8?
   b   an addition of D5 to D8?
   c   a subtraction of D5 from D8?
   d   a multiplication of D5 and D8?

22 Which ONE of the following is an example of the use of a process control system?

   a   financial control of business expenses using a spreadsheet
   b   quality control of commercial documents using a spellcheck facility

   c   environmental control in a power plant by monitoring pollution levels
   d   staffing control in a factory by checking staff attendance sheets.

Questions 23 and 24 are related to Text 2.

> *Text 2*
> In a pottery, a process control system is used for the heating of the kiln.

23 In a control system, which of the following stages would check that the temperature in the kiln is kept at a constant temperature?

   a   sense inputs
   b   adjust output
   c   calculate action
   d   compare conditions.

24 In a control system, which of the following stages would ensure that the kiln does not become too hot or fall below the pre-set limits?

   a   sense inputs
   b   adjust output
   c   calculate action
   d   compare conditions.

25 In addition to using sensors in intruder alarms and fire alarms, they can also be used in cameras. Such sensors are known as which ONE of the following?

   a   light and proximity devices
   b   processor controls
   c   control procedure
   d   output devices.

26 In a dishwasher, the processor would perform which ONE of the following tasks?

   a   ensure the dishes are stacked safely

b select the correct temperature of
water for the given program
c ensure the dishwasher is not
overloaded
d ensure the dishes are cleaned.

27 Traffic lights use a control procedure.
Which ONE of the following tasks
would they perform?

a sense the number of cars passing
b sense the type of car passing
c sense the colour of the cars passing
d sense the make of the cars passing.

28 The speakers on a television regulate
the volume of sound in the room by use
of which ONE of the following?

a control procedure
b sensors
c output devices
d input devices.

29 Interconnecting devices connect the
different components in a process
control system. They do this by using
which ONE of the following?

a signals and sensors
b output devices
c input devices
d control procedures.

element

3.1

Examine the flow of information in organisations

Identify different types of organisation, and give examples

It is probably easier to think of a specific example of a business organisation than it is to try to define what a business organisation actually is. Although, as we will see, business organisations can differ enormously, they do have some common features:

- they often use resources that are in limited supply – such as human resources, money and materials
- they provide something – either a product or a service
- they normally compete with other organisations.

Each organisation must undertake a wide variety of different tasks or functions to ensure that it operates well within the area

it is involved in. Some of these functions include:

- *managing employees* – usually through a personnel (or human resources) department
- *selling products or services* – providing the customer with the product or service which he/she requires
- *distributing the product or service* – ensuring that the customer has access to what he/she needs
- *purchasing products or services* – ordering stock for either short-term use or long-term needs
- *marketing a product or service* – researching the customers' needs and then promoting the product or service
- *keeping financial records* – to monitor the success of the organisation.

Also, organisations must ensure, when they need to make a choice, that they make the correct decision. A wide variety of considerations may have an impact on this decision, including the use of resources which may be limited, so the organisation must ensure that it makes the right decision as often as possible.

Business organisations do not always have the same objective. Perhaps the most common, as we will see later, is the profit motive, but not all organisations are driven by this goal.

Commercial organisations

A **commercial organisation** is one whose primary function is to purchase and sell goods and services, and to make a profit.

Industrial or manufacturing organisations

An **industrial** or **manufacturing organisation** primarily exists to construct, assemble or otherwise make a product. It is during this process (known as the **production process**) than an organisation **adds value** to the raw materials or components that it began the process with, and eventually ends up creating some form of finished good. This production process can take many forms. For example:

- a car-tyre manufacturer uses rubber during the production process to produce car tyres. However, the final selling price of the car tyres is far in excess of the original cost of the rubber. In other words, during the production process, the added-value aspect makes the rubber (in its new form as car tyres) more valuable
- a furniture manufacturer constructing

various items from wood (or lumber) will similarly put its raw materials through a series of production processes to make tables, chairs, desks etc. Again, the value of the wood after it has gone through the production process is significantly greater than the value of the tree from which it came.

student activity

● **COM** 2.2
Make a list of at least 10 manufacturing organisations that you can think of. What raw materials would they use?

Factors determining the production method

In any industry, there are universally accepted methods of production. However, there are also many other factors which determine an organisation's choice of production method. These determinants include:

- available investment
- the target customer (perhaps the organisation is producing hand-made products for the more wealthy customer)
- the availability of skilled labour
- the availability of affordable and applicable machinery
- the availability of raw materials (these raw materials may be complete 'raw' or part-processed already)
- location (this is particularly true of organisations manufacturing goods in the Third World).

The scale of production (in other words, how many products the organisation produces) is also an important determinant of the way an organisation operates. Larger-scale production can mean cheaper raw materials and more efficient methods of production. Obviously, the higher the production level, the more the organisation in turn desires higher productivity levels, and therefore higher levels of efficiency, from its employees.

Location

Location has already been mentioned, and any organisation that wishes to do more than survive in a competitive market must take great care in choosing the siting of its factories. Great economies can be made by being located either close to the source of raw materials (e.g. to where the raw materials are grown or mined) or where the raw materials can at least be easily accessed (via good transportation links). Equally, an organisation should be aware that it can avoid certain costs by being close to the market in which it wishes to sell its finished goods.

Public-service organisations

Despite large-scale privatisation, there still exist numerous organisations which provide a **public service** in some form. Primarily, these include:

- central government departments
- local authorities
- quangos (quasi-autonomous nongovernmental organisations, appointed by the government to provide certain services)
- directly or indirectly funded organisations (such as hospitals and colleges)
- specialist organisations (such as those set up to advise businesses and direct certain government initiatives).

In the past, many public services were that in name only: they did provide a service but they were not necessarily accountable or responsive to public needs. However, recent government legislation now requires them to be accessible, responsive and efficient.

Some of the key public-service considerations include:

- *providing benefits and grants* – organisations such as the Department of Social Security (DSS) or councils are responsible for providing a range of benefits and grants, either to the unemployed or to students. In this respect, the public-service aspect of the organisation is obvious, though there are less obvious ways in which some public-sector organisations can also provide vital services
- *providing advice and guidance* – councils and central government, through a variety of different sub-organisations, provide a vast range of support services to industries and individuals. These services include business advice and guidance through the Department of Trade and Industry (DTI), and more local support for business via the Chamber of Commerce. Individuals can obtain useful advice on demand through the Citizen's Advice Bureau that are common in nearly all towns and cities
- *collection and monitoring* – the Inland Revenue not only collects income tax and other forms of taxation based on profits from business, but also provides useful business advice concerning financial control and monitoring
- *Customs and Excise* – this department is not only responsible for the collection and monitoring of VAT (value-added tax) but also provides useful guidelines for the collection, payment and monitoring of this 'sales tax'
- *data collection* – many central government departments routinely collect data which is of great use to

businesses. Data is readily available on employment trends, family expenditure, growth or decline in markets, and exports.

Describe the internal and external functions of a specified organisation

Describe the types of information used in a specified organisation

Systems, and efficiency and effectiveness

The **systems** which an organisation has in place should aim to establish a means by which the efficiency and effectiveness of all operations are assessed. All systems rely on the way in which an organisation is structured and on the comparative degree of importance with which individuals within the organisation view those systems.

Any system is only a series of sub-systems which themselves may be split into additional sub-systems. It is therefore important that an organisation monitor all parts of the system. The systems should be designed in such a way that they can be amended or can evolve to meet the requirements of the organisation. In order to understand the ways in which organisations work, we need to understand how they can assess the efficiency and effectiveness of all their operations.

Effectiveness is concerned with how an organisation achieves its objectives. At its simplest, if an organisation meets its declared objectives, then it is being effective. However, the amount of resources deployed to achieve these goals,

i.e. the degree of efficiency involved in the operation, should also be measured in order to assess effectiveness. We cannot therefore assess how successful an organisation is simply by considering efficiency or effectiveness separately: an organisation needs to operate both efficiently and effectively, and its operations need to be coordinated. Even if only one part of an organisation fails in its task, then we cannot state that the organisation is truly efficient or effective. One or more features in the organisation's systems must be deficient if one part of the organisation is under-achieving.

O & M Analysis

Systems obviously play a vital role here. They are the means by which an organisation is able to operate as a whole entity. Any organisation can have good ideas and well-motivated personnel, but without systems to ensure that vital functions are carried out, these may be doomed to failure. Organisations need not necessarily rely on their own personnel to provide the design and running of systems. They may employ outside specialists or consultants who are conversant with **Organisation and Methods (O & M)**

Analysis. In recent years, indeed, many organisations have employed this vital tool to improve efficiency and effectiveness. Whether the systems of an organisation evolve from existing systems or are radically redesigned, O & M bases its assessment on a scientific analysis. Systems are vital to measure the performance of an organisation and to assess whether it is reaching its declared objectives. However the systems have originated, they will always be open to criticism and to the charge of being responsible for inefficiencies or ineffectiveness.

Internal functions of an organisation, with types of information used

As we have said, the running of an organisation requires an organised approach if it is to be efficient and effective. Administrative tasks will be carried out at all levels of an organisation. In a larger organisation, there will be a separate **administration department**, but in smaller businesses a single individual may be responsible for all forms of administration. Whatever the set-up, the basic purposes of administrative procedures remain the same:

- to provide support systems for all resources used by the organisation
- to keep records relating to the activities of the organisation
- to monitor the performance of the business's activities.

Finance

Budgetary control
The main function of **accounting systems** is to provide managers with the means to exercise financial control over their departments. A **budget** relies on a plan which is made on the basis of estimates of future spending and income. A budget will also try to allocate any expenses in relation to particular objectives set by the organisation. Depending upon the size of the organisation, this allocation may occur across the whole of the organisation or on a departmental basis. Budgetary control is established by careful consideration of the following:

- the organisation will define its objectives and try to allocate the expenditure related to each of them
- the organisation will establish **standard operating procedures** which relate to specific strategies and tactics carried out to meet the objectives
- the organisation will establish systems to monitor actual – as opposed to estimated – spending on each objective
- the above monitoring of the objectives in relation to the standards set will be made at various times, and may take the form of **interim reports**
- the organisation must have in place a series of procedures enabling it to react to any differences between estimated and actual spending levels. This is particularly important if there is overexpenditure, and the result may be a re-examination of the organisation's operating systems. Most organisations, indeed, will expect to have to constantly redefine their operating standards and monitoring systems in order to maintain efficiency.

The accurate monitoring of budgets is essential to all businesses for the following reasons:

- it allows the organisation to clearly define its aims and policies
- it allows the organisation to develop an overall **corporate strategy**
- it allows the key decision-makers of the organisation to keep a careful eye on all budgets

- it allows the organisation to monitor actual performance against estimated activity
- it should improve the organisation's level of efficiency and allow a more effective deployment of resources towards meeting specific objectives.

Credit matters

Concerning the creditworthiness of a customer, most organisations will have set a particular policy at high management level. In large organisations, there may be one individual with specific responsibility for **credit control** and the setting of customers' credit levels. In smaller organisations, as we have mentioned, an individual may have to take on this responsibility in addition to other tasks. But in any case, an efficient credit system should include the following features:

- *credit checks* – which include the taking up of bank and trade references and references from credit agencies
- *the establishment of credit levels* – and of the terms that apply to these limits
- *action to be taken in the case of credit breaches* – a system is created to determine at what particular stage action will be taken. It will include a series of letters requesting payment. The style and tone of these letters is important in order to avoid unnecessary

student activity

- **COM** 2.2
- **IT** 2.1

Design and write a letter aimed at obtaining an outstanding debt from a customer. Bear in mind that you should always be clear and courteous. Word process your letter and print two copies.

complications, both legally and personally, with the customer
- *credit ratings* – which are often based on sales experience with a particular customer. Credit ratings given to customers should reflect their ability to pay at some point in the future.

Main points

Specifically, then, the major requirements of the administrative system with a **finance** or **accounts department** are:

- to record information
- to store records either manually or by using a database or specific accounts software
- to have these records available for inspection by the Inland Revenue (for tax purposes)
- to have these records available for inspection by Customs and Excise (for VAT purposes)
- to have these records available for inspection by the company's auditors
- to report on the financial health of the organisation at the end of the year.

It is vital that these systems work as the organisation will need them for the following:

- planning
- decision-making
- financial control.

It is usual, particularly in larger organisations, that the **chief accountant** (or equivalent) be a member of the **board of directors**.

Operations and operations information

The **production department** is involved in all functions which revolve around producing goods or services for the customer. This department monitors levels of wastage to ensure the most efficient use of resources, and checks the cost of raw materials and parts purchased to make sure that **profit margins** are maintained.

As new products are developed and technology changes, the production department will be responsible for purchasing all the necessary plant and equipment required, as well as for organising the production process.

Purchasing

All organisations need to buy products and services to make other goods to sell or to provide the service from which they make their profits. A **purchasing department** – which will deal with **invoices** and **orders** – is responsible for buying the following:

- raw materials from which they make their products to sell
- components or part-finished goods from which they make their products to sell
- finished products which they sell
- goods which they require in order to run their business, e.g. office stationery and furniture
- the services of a cleaning company or interior designer
- the services of an accountant or auditor
- the services of a solicitor
- the services of a bank.

Sales and marketing

Sales department

The **sales department** relates to those parts of the organisation which have direct contact with the customer. In this instance, we also include the **marketing function**, since this may have a responsibility for **customer service** in terms of advertising, promotion and quality assurance. The exact relationship between sales and marketing will very much depend upon the organisation itself.

The key functions of sales staff are to control and organise the selling and distribution of an organisation's products and services. The sales function may often be found within the marketing department of an organisation, but the sales operation will always be supported by administrative personnel and various sales representatives. As with any other managerial function, the **sales manager** will be responsible for the establishment and revision of systems which will ensure the smooth running of the sales operation. In addition, he/she may have specific targets to meet and must maintain budgetary control over these. Communication is a key feature of a good sales department, as the staff must be able to handle all interaction with customers. They will also be responsible for the maintenance of any relevant records, and will exercise some control (via a credit controller) over the availability of credit to customers.

Marketing department

The main function of the **marketing department** is to try to identify customer requirements. There is also an element of trying to predict customer needs into the future. The marketing department works very closely with the sales department, and it is important that the two communicate well.

The starting point for most marketing functions is to carry out extensive research on a particular market to try to discover exactly what customers want, where they want it, how much they want to pay for it and the most effective way of getting the message across. This is known as the **marketing mix**. The marketing department will need to work closely with the **research and development (R&D)** department and the production department in developing attractive and sellable products. This work will also include the constant updating of existing products to cater for changes in taste and demand. As a part of its regular **market research** procedures, the marketing department will monitor changes in trends and fashions that affect the organisation's customers. Some information is readily available as statistical tables published by the government, but much information must also be researched as required by the organisation itself.

One of the more obvious responsibilities of the marketing department is the design and development of advertising ideas and **marketing campaigns**. This design and development process will take account of the needs both of the sales department and of any other interested area of the organisation.

External functions of an organisation

Customers

Organisational criteria
Whether an organisation is producing goods or providing a service, there are still certain criteria which it will have to meet on a regular basis. For organisations providing services only (not manufacturing goods), the following requirements would be equally important and would be carried out on a regular basis by the administration systems in place within that organisation. These requirements include:

- the organisation must be ready, willing and able to provide a wide variety of information instantly and on demand. Its meetings (particularly if it is in the public sector) must be open to the public, and information packs should be available on request
- the organisation must be fully aware of how much a customer would be willing to pay for its service
- the organisation must be fully aware of how much it is costing to provide the

service. Costs could include the following:
  - premises
  - workforce costs
  - development costs
  - training costs
  - cleaning costs
  - administration costs
- costs can be either short-term or long-term. Short-term costs tend to be fairly fixed in the sense that it is difficult here to change the level of expenditure in a short period of time. If an organisation providing a service needs to respond financially to sudden changes in the market, then it may be unable to find the additional funding required. Long-term costs, on the other hand, tend to be more variable. These costs will be incurred whether the organisation is producing goods or not. Therefore, administration systems need to be in place to monitor these costs
- the organisation must be aware both of the competition within the market it is dealing in and of the price these competitors are charging
- the organisation must be aware of the quality of service its competitors are providing
- the organisation must ensure that the service it is providing is constantly monitored with regard to efficiency, effectiveness and quality.

Customer-service administration
Dealing with customers requires the establishment of systems to deal efficiently with problems and enquiries. These systems will also require the sales department to keep records of any enquiries made, of orders received and of other documentation needed to maintain an up-to-date record of customer transactions.

When sales staff have contact with customers, whether this is by telephone or personal visit, administration systems must be in place to ensure that the details of any conservation, negotiation or problems have been recorded accurately. This information will be held by the sales department, and will include many of the following:

- the name and phone number of the customer's **chief buyer**
- the discounts agreed
- the creditworthiness of the customer
- specific customer requirements
- delivery arrangements
- the size of the customer order
- the frequency of the customer order.

student activity

- **COM** 2.2
- **AON** 2.1

Design a form which would be appropriate for the recording of the above data. Compare your form to those of your peers.

The documentation and administration systems used by the **customer service** wing of an organisation will very much depend upon the nature of the organisation itself. In general, however, areas covered by the systems will include:

- the processing of sales information (through invoices/order forms and letters etc.)
- marketing research (including data-collection and analysis)
- customer-care details (guarantees/warranties etc.) and customer service (dealing with complaints etc.)
- sales promotions (i.e. all non-advertising marketing such as special offers etc.)
- advertising (planning, monitoring etc.)

- support services (via personnel for training and development etc.)
- general sales administration.

F OCUS STUDY

Customer service

Many retailers, hoteliers and restaurant chains have used 'under-cover' customers to assess how their outlets and staff perform. The concept of the 'mystery shopper' has now moved to the financial institutions of banks and building societies. The high-street banks and building societies are very worried about their image. They have a low standing in public opinion and want to turn this around. In 1994–95, some £2 million will be spent by them on 'mystery shopper' surveys to assess their staffs' ability to respond to customers' needs and problems. The TSB itself is expected to spend some £200,000, but does not want the operation to be seen as a method of weeding out staff who do not come up to scratch. LAUTRO (to be replaced by the Personnel Investment Authority), the regulator of life and unit trust companies, also uses 'mystery shoppers' to test members' levels of training, competence and ability to cope with customer demands.

Suppliers

The suppliers of the organisation are those individuals or organisations whom the purchasing department buys from. A good relationship with suppliers is as important as good relationships between different departments of an organisation. A good supplier will ultimately determine whether or not the organisation is efficient and effective, and this could result in a profit being made or lost. Obviously, an organisation has a choice. If it finds that the service it is receiving from its regular supplier is deteriorating, then it can shop around to find an alternative. However, this could result in a loss of orders if the goods being bought are held up while the new supplier is being established.

Produce a diagram to show the flow of information between functions

For the purposes of this performance criteria, you have to produce, by means of information technology, a diagram which shows that you understand how information passes between the different departments of an organisation. In Figure 3.1.1, we give you one example of a diagram which can show this flow of information, but you will need to take instruction from your teacher/tutor as to how this task will fit into the other activities you will be carrying out during your course of study.

THE INPUT
incoming messages in the form of: memos, telephone calls, fax transmissions, electronic mail transmissions

↓

THE PROCESSING
entering data into a computer system: spreadsheet, database or word processing, entering information into a diary or making an appointment

↓

THE OUTPUT
feedback to the initial input by means of: electronic mail, fax message, telephone call, sending of written document, meeting of individuals

FIGURE 3.1.1 *A diagram showing the flow of information through an organisation*

assignment

For the purposes of providing evidence for this performance criteria, you must produce a report which includes all of the tasks we give below:

task 1

This first task requires you to identify the different types of organisation, giving two examples of each type.

task 2

The next part of your report should describe the functions of one particular organisation.

task 3

The final part of your report should describe the types of information used in your particular organisation.

task 4

Finally, you should attach to your report a flow chart which shows the flow of information between all the internal and external functions of your particular organisation.

● NOTES

The one particular organisation that you choose should be agreed with your teacher/tutor. It could be one that you visit and research as a group, or it could be your work-placement company or one for which you work on a part-time basis.

3.2

Describe data-handling systems

3.2.1

Describe methods of information processing and types of data-handling system

Methods of processing

Once information or data has been inputted into a computer, it is then necessary for that information to be processed. There are two main methods of processing information, and we look at both of these under the next two range statements.

Batch processing

The **batch processing** of data is a method of processing used when the information is not required urgently. It is usual for the operator to process the data as one job, and the method is used for large amounts of data. Obviously, accuracy is vital, as is the guarantee that none of the data will be lost. The system will be set up in such a way that thousands of data entries can be inputted into the computer without any

direct interaction between the operator and the system. In this way, it is possible for batch processing to take place at night or at the weekends.

Batch processing will be used:

- for large amounts of non-urgent data
- for regularly processed data
- when all the data is ready to be inputted before the batch is processed
- when there is no need for operator interaction as the program is set up in such a way as to deal with the routine data.

Batch processing is normally carried out on **mainframe computers**, and the following procedures are involved:

- the data is checked to ensure that the information is accurate and complete
- the documents are sorted into batches

- the operator makes a list of all the batches (usually on **proforma** documents)
- totals are calculated manually for each of the batches
- the data is entered onto the computer in 'record mode' and saved
- the data is then entered onto the computer in 'verify mode'
- any discrepancies between 'record mode' and 'verify mode' are highlighted by the computer and amended by the input clerk. This process is known as **verification**, and once the entries have been verified, it is almost guaranteed that no further errors are likely
- the work is then saved (in a transition file), and the computer will process it once it reaches this stage in the queue
- the data is then stored to disk and printed.

Batch processing will tend to be used by large companies who have thousands of customers, good examples being British Gas and the electricity boards.

Transaction processing

The alternative to batch processing is **transaction processing**. This will tend to be used where information is processed immediately by the operator, with direct contact with the computer. Transaction processing normally takes place on mainframe computers with the use of large databases, and will be used:

- with small amounts of data
- where information has to be completely up-to-date
- where each piece of data is inputted as it arrives at the organisation, as opposed to weekly or monthly.

Typical examples of organisations using this method are airports, travel agents, hotels and restaurants. They will use this system so that overbooking errors are avoided and because their customers want immediate confirmation that their request has been processed.

Types of data-handling system

We look in this section at the various types of **data-handling system** in operation. Obviously, the different types will be used for a variety of different reasons. A wide variety of data-handling systems can be bought in by an organisation; or it can have one made for it, which is obviously more expensive and also means less readily available assistance should anything go wrong. An organisation will require its data-handling systems to have the following facilities:

- *the ability to hold 'constant' information* – which will include information which does not change very often. Examples of constant information are:
  - employee records – where only the name or address or telephone numbers are likely to change infrequently, if at all.
  - customer records – again where there are likely to be only minor changes to the data
- *variable data* – which could change daily or weekly. Such data will include the overtime worked by employees or the price of products held in stock.

Bookings

As we have already mentioned, travel agents, hoteliers, airlines and restaurants will use their data-handling system for making **bookings**. This information will have to be constantly up-to-date so that errors are avoided in their booking procedures. Travel agents may need their data to be available throughout the world. Regardless of whether the booking system used is for local, national or international use, it will have to be capable of recording the following information:

- the name of the person who has made the booking
- the purpose of the booking
- the date the booking was made
- the dates for which the booking is required.

For a large organisation such as an airline, the booking system will have to be much more sophisticated and capable of ensuring the following:

- it must have a central computer which holds complete details of all bookings made
- it must be able to take bookings using different methods (e.g. in person at the airline, via the travel agent or over the telephone)
- it must be able to communicate with the different terminals which are also accepting bookings
- it must be able to store all the information – the times, availability and cost of all the different flights
- it must be able to accept bookings and amend the flight-availability information contained on the computer
- it must be able to refuse the booking if the flight becomes full
- it must be able to accept any cancellations and consequently amend the flight-availability information contained on the central computer
- it must be able to prepare and print tickets
- it must be able to register the names of the passengers.

Payrolls

Employees of an organisation are paid in a variety of ways: by cash, by cheque or directly into their bank account by **bank transfer**. A computerised **payroll** system – as already discussed in Element 1.1 on

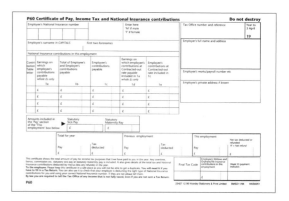

FIGURE 3.2.1 *An example of a P60*

pages 8–9 – must be able to calculate and print out the following:

- the employee's gross pay (the amount he/she has earned before any deductions have been made)
- the amount of tax the employee must pay
- the amount of national insurance contributions the employee must pay
- the amount of pension contributions the employee must pay
- the employee's net pay (the amount he/she actually receives once the deductions have been made)
- cheques, details for the bank of salaries being paid by bank transfer and pay slips
- P60s (which are issued at the end of the tax year in April) showing the tax paid and national insurance contributions for the tax year
- P45s (which are issued to employees when they leave the organisation to take alternative employment)
- a total list of all taxes paid for the Inland Revenue at the end of the tax period.

Ordering

The processing of **orders** can be simplified by the use of computers – it can be a very complex process. In order to successfully process orders to ensure that an organisation maintains sufficient supplies, there has to be some degree of forward planning. In most organisations, purchases have to be authorised by named individuals. Usually, this will be someone in authority, perhaps in the accounts department. Once a **purchase order requisition** has been completed and signed, the purchasing department, or an individual responsible for placing orders, takes over the task. In most cases, the purchase requisition form will have very clear instructions as to what is required. This will mean that the person responsible for placing the order has a relatively easy task as he/she will probably know whom to buy from and the rough price. For more complicated purchases, or in cases where the purchase requisition form is not very detailed, the person responsible for purchasing may have to go back to the originator of the form to check details or specifications.

Not only will the purchase requisition form be dated in terms of when the order was requested, there may also be a date relating to the latest required delivery time. This will give the person responsible for purchasing some idea of the degree of urgency of the order. It may be possible for the purchaser to combine this order with another order from another department in order to cut down on delivery costs or to obtain a higher rate of discount.

Once the organisation's buyer has looked at all of the possibilities which meet the requirements of the purchase order, he/she will then be able to select the appropriate product and issue a **purchase order** (see Figure 3.2.2). This can be made in writing, by fax, by telephone or by electronic transfer. The order itself will, of course, include the exact specifications of the product(s) required, the desired delivery date and any other conditions relating to the order. The supplier will require some form of authorisation from the purchasing organisation, and this may

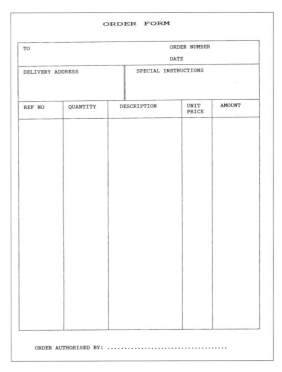

FIGURE 3.2.2 *An example of an order form which would be completed and sent to a supplier by the purchasing department of an organisation*

be a purchase order number or perhaps a signature from an authorised individual. The buyer will also have to send one copy of the order to the accounts department (to ensure that this department can check it against the invoice when it arrives) and a further copy to the warehouse or delivery point (so that they know to expect the order and to whom it should be sent).

Normally, the supplier will acknowledge the order to enable the buyer to check that the details are correct. This will also confirm that the supplier has received the order. A **delivery note** will accompany the goods, and this will clearly state exactly what has been supplied (see Figure 3.2.3). The supplier will expect that someone from the purchasing organisation will sign a declaration that the correct goods have been delivered in a suitable state. Given

DELIVERY NOTE

TO

NUMBER

YOUR ORDER NUMBER

DATE

THE FOLLOWING ITEMS HAVE BEEN DESPATCHED TODAY TO ________

________________ BY RAIL/COMPANY VAN/POST*

QUANTITY	DESCRIPTION	NUMBER OF PACKAGES

I certify that the goods received have been checked and are in good condition

Signed: .... On behalf of: ....

Date: ....

I certify that the number of packages delivered is correct according to the number stated above, but that the goods have not been checked

Signed: .... On behalf of: ....

Date: ....

FIGURE 3.2.3 *An example of a delivery note*

GOODS RECEIVED NOTE

NO	DATE RECEIVED	ORDER NO	DELIVERED BY
QUANTITY	DESCRIPTION	NUMBER OF PACKAGES	STORES REF

RECEIVED FROM	ENTERED INTO STOCK		RECEIVED BY
	DATE	INITIAL	
SUPPLIER			STOREKEEPER

FIGURE 3.2.4 *An example of a goods received note*

that the majority of deliveries are made by an independent carrier, this is extremely important as this could be a potential problem in the delivery process. The purchasing organisation would need to tell the supplier immediately if there is a problem with the order.

As a further internal check, the purchasing organisation will now produce a **goods received note** (see Figure 3.2.4). This is a way in which the organisation can record that the delivery has been accepted. Copies will be sent to the accounts department and the purchasing department. In this way, both departments now know that the delivery has been received.

In organisations which have fully integrated computerised systems, the goods will now be entered onto the stock records. At the same time, confirmation can be made by email or another internal system to inform the accounts and purchasing department of the delivery.

Invoicing

Computers can be used to make **invoicing** far more efficient, as well as to keep a check on a number of different considerations related to the fulfilment of orders:

- the checking of the **credit status** of the customer to ensure that goods are not sent to customers who owe the organisation outstanding invoices or who have reached their credit limit
- the checking and identification of individual products ordered by the customer so that a 'picking list' can be generated for the warehouse in order to simplify the packing of the order
- the checking and monitoring of **back orders** so that products which could not

be sent to the customer from a previous order can now be added to the current order

- the automatic reduction of stock levels – which should trigger re-ordering when the stock level reaches the minimum stock level.

An invoice will be raised for the goods supplied and sent to the purchasing organisation. This will either be included with the delivery or sent separately soon after. As we saw when we considered ordering, the purchasing organisation will be able to check the invoice against the original order and goods received note to verify the details before authorising payment.

Figure 2.1.3 on page 46 of Element 2.1 shows an example of a completed invoice.

Stock control

For organisations which hold a wide variety of different products in stock, a reliable system is needed to manage and monitor stock levels. Some organisations will need to ensure that stock levels are maintained at a sufficiently high level to be able to supply customers' immediate demands. Other organisations may need to have stock levels of consumable items (such as paper, printer cartridges and envelopes) that will be used by the organisation itself. In order to do this, accurate stock records will be needed to monitor the movement of stock in and out of the organisation, as well as to establish minimum and maximum stock levels.

Stock records usually take the form of a **stock record card**. This will monitor the movement of stock, relying on the accurate recording both of new stocks received and of the distribution of stock internally or externally. With the internal movement of stock, receipts will have to be signed by the departments upon acceptance of the goods. This in effect works in a very similar way

to recording the acceptance of an order. It will be someone's responsibility to record the transaction, calculate the new stock balance and check that the minimum re-order level has not been reached. If the latter has happened, then an order will need to be placed to replenish the stock above the minimum re-order level.

An efficient stock-control system should be able to perform the following:

- record the cost of all products in stock
- record the price of all products in stock
- trigger an order if the stock level has dropped to the minimum re-order level
- alert the organisation to serious overstocking.

By carefully monitoring stock levels, an organisation will be able to identify the pattern of sales, the use of particular products, those products which are not 'moving well' and whether there are any overdue orders. For accounting purposes, all stock is classed as an **asset**. In other words, if the organisation wished, it could turn the stock into cash.

Personnel records

Organisations, by law, need to be very careful about the information that they keep on computer regarding their employees. Above all, this information needs to be confidential and kept in a secure environment. We look in more detail at government legislation which controls the storing of personnel information in Element 3.4 of this book.

Apart from the payroll details which will have to be maintained by the personnel department, there will also be information regarding holiday entitlements, sick leave taken, qualifications of employees and any training they have undertaken. For this reason, any information of a personal nature held by an organisation will have to be secure and only available to a limited number of key personnel.

3.2.2

Describe the objectives of a specified data-handling system

As you will see, the assignment for this element requires you to look at a specific data-handling system. The objectives of the system which you choose will probably be obvious since the majority of such systems have instantly recognisable purposes. It would be impossible to describe all of the objectives of different data-handling systems, so in this performance criteria we will give you a series of points, corresponding to the range statements, which you can focus on in order to describe a specific data-handling system.

Accuracy

Given the fact that any computerised system is only as accurate as the data it receives, there is always the possibility that the information is inaccurate as a result of human error. Obviously, more sophisticated data-handling systems will have a series of checks and double-checks in order to identify potential errors. Accuracy is of paramount importance if the organisation is to rely upon the system, especially given that many decisions will be made on the basis of the information that it handles. You will need to assess whether the system is foolproof and accurate in most cases.

Cost

Most organisations will use data-handling systems in order to cut costs. Bearing in mind that there will be significant costs related to the initial purchasing and setting up of the system, there needs to be a point at which the data-handling system gives good value for money as far as the organisation is concerned. This can be measured in terms of either the time that can be saved in using the system or the reduction in the number of employees. At other times, cost-cutting benefits could also include the fact that sales are not lost, goods are always in stock, or employees are paid the correct amount in salary. The more time that can be saved by not having to repeat tasks or sort out problems, the more money that will be saved.

Speed

In most cases, the use of data-handling systems means that information can be processed much faster than it could using a manual system. Provided they can rely on the system, as we have already seen, employees are freed to concentrate on customer service issues or the development of new services. Many organisations have to operate within very strict deadlines, particularly in the banking sector where many millions of financial transactions have to be processed in the same day. This would be impossible if carried out manually. There is still some manual input, but the majority of the work is now carried out by the data-handling system.

Support decision-making

As we have said earlier, provided an organisation can rely upon the speed and accuracy of its data-handling system, it will be able to make informed decisions far more easily. Data-handling systems can be used at all levels to aid decision-making. Depending on the system used, the buyer will be able to concentrate on obtaining goods at the best possible price, the accountant will be able to decide in which order invoices should be paid, the area

manager will be able to make a judgement about the sales of each of the retail shops in the area, or the managing director will be able to look at the performance of a new product or service. The use of data-handling systems is vital in order to ensure that employees and managers can spend more time on issues which are not related to simple routine tasks.

Describe data sources for a specified data-handling system

Describe methods of data capture for a specified data-handling system

Data sources

Having chosen your data-handling system, you will now have to consider the sources of the data which the system uses and how it captures this information. There are, of course, a number of choices which we will investigate in these two performance criteria. Some will be more or less relevant to your own chosen data-handling system. Remember that not all data-capture methods necessarily involve a great deal of human input.

Bar codes

Using a combination of thick and thin lines, a **bar code** is able to give a coded representation of data. Bar codes can now be found in a wide variety of different retail outlets and warehouses, and have the following features:

- they are often an integral part of the packaging

FIGURE 3.2.5 *Some examples of bar codes*

- each product has its own unique code
- they can be used with another bar code, such as with the issuing of books in a library
- in addition to registering the sale of a product, they can automatically reduce the stock level by one
- they can also be used to form the basis of an order by registering the bar code and then inputting the number to be ordered from the supplier.

Documents

Obviously, not all organisations with whom a purchaser or supplier deals are up-to-date in their use of computerised systems, and inevitably, information will often have to be transferred from more conventional documents onto the purchaser's or supplier's own data-handling system. This is particularly true of situations such as:

- the setting up of customer files or records from handwritten forms detailing the name, address and telephone number of each customer
- the transfer of orders from pre-printed order forms or from telephone orders
- the updating of personnel records to include new details such as a change of address
- the amendment of product specification as a result of information received from the supplier.

student activity

● **COM** 2.1, 2.2

In pairs, list the other documentation which could be used as data for inputting into a data-handling system.

Electronic files

An efficient data-handling system will have the capacity to allow users to transfer whole files of data held electronically from one system to another, so that the information can then be used for a variety of different purposes. A bank which has a cash-dispensing machine will need to be able to capture information regarding transactions and then transfer that information to individual customer records, as well as to a more general log of branch activity.

Similarly, it is possible to transfer electronic files from one remote system to another through Electronic Data Interchange (EDI). Here, it is possible to download files via a telephone connection with another system so that information can be used immediately in another location.

People

Many marketing organisations which operate research and data-gathering activities on behalf of clients have extremely sophisticated data-capture systems. By means of telephone interviews, operators are able to ask questions and immediately input information gained onto a screen. In this way, the information can be analysed without having to be separately inputted at a later date.

Many questionnaires contain a series of codes which act as prompts for operators to input certain values or numbers instead of longhand data. Each response on the questionnaire will be allotted a particular code number, and in this way the operator is able to input a large number of questionnaires in a relatively short period of time. This again also means that the data is immediately available and can be analysed straight away.

Methods of data capture

Bar-code readers

To register a bar code, an operator needs to use a **bar-code reader**, which he/she swipes across the bar code, and this forms the major part of the data capture. In most cases, read-errors are low, and the whole procedure is again much quicker than any manual system.

Keyboard

There was a time when the keyboard was the primary means by which data could be entered onto any system. This, of course, relies on the skill of the keyboard operator. However, since the majority of keyboard input is repetitive, systems have now developed which enable an operator to take a number of short cuts by using repetitive keystrokes (we looked at this system of setting up macros in Element 1.4). Not only does this radically improve the efficiency of the keyboard operator, it also means that the risk of **repetitive strain injury (RSI)** (see Element 3.4, page 121) is reduced. It is still the case that the majority of keyboard operators are comparatively unskilled. Not only this, the number of errors likely to occur through manual input is still high.

Magnetic reader

The **magnetic reader** was one of the first attempts at automating data entry, and it is used extensively in banking. Characters are printed on cheques or other documents with an ink that has the ability to be magnetised. The reader then recognises each magnetised character, thus enabling the system to be automated. This system has been superseded by **optical character recognition**, which allows characters to be scanned from a document and then stored within a computer system

Mouse

The mouse is used essentially as a control device. Using the mouse to point and click enables an operator to reduce the number of commands that need to be entered via the keyboard. This also means that operators who do not have a high level of computer or keyboard skills can still input information and manipulate data.

Sensor

There are a number of data-capture systems in development that are related to sensors, and these include the ability to collect data regarding the movement of vehicles and individuals. Many busy cities and toll motorways are considering using sensors to capture data regarding the ownership of vehicles using their highways. In this way, they can then bill the owner of the vehicle on the basis of the level of use. There have also been a number of pilot schemes involving putting a tag around the ankles of convicted criminals who have been placed under **house arrest** rather than conventional imprisonment. The tags are monitored and picked up by the sensors if the individual strays out of his/her designated area.

3.2.5

Describe processes applied to data in specified data-handling systems

In data-handling systems, most data is held in the form of **records**. These can be stored on either magnetic disk or magnetic tape. As we have seen, databases comprise a series of related **files**. All data is stored by the computer in a code, and the codes can be ranked according to value. Normally, an alpha-numeric string or data field occurs in each record or file, allowing the user to rank or sequence that file. This is what enables a computer to sequence the files according to instructions given by an operator. Depending on the data-handling system concerned, the computer will manipulate the data in a number of different ways, and these will include calculations, searches, selection, sorting and validating. Let us now consider each of these in turn.

Calculating

There are a number of different ways in which a programmer can instruct software to carry out a series of calculations. Normally, the software of a data-handling system will only be able to recognise that it needs to make a series of calculations if the arithmetic data is inputted accurately and in the correct format. A good example of the way in which inputted data can be manipulated by the use of a computer is found with spreadsheet software (which we have already considered in some detail in Element 2.3. of this book). By the use of appropriate formulae, it is possible to instruct a computer to add, subtract, divide and multiply numerical data within a spreadsheet. These simple calculations allow the user to produce detailed

information either in tabulated form or by the use of graphic images such as pie or bar charts and line graphs.

Searching and selecting

By the use of a search or select facility, it is possible to look through files or records and choose particular ones. This is obviously a much quicker process than the older manual methods. Search and select facilities will be used:

- in order to find particular information or to check the availability of, say, a booking or order
- in order to answer a particular query on an invoice
- in order to find specific information on one individual, e.g. his/her address
- in order to find specific information regarding all those individuals who work in a particular area of a business; e.g. the ages of those who work in one branch of a retail outlet.

Sorting

Sorting files or records means putting them in a particular group or in the same category. In other words, it means putting records into a particular order, e.g.:

- *in alphabetical order* – with those beginning with 'A' going first, i.e. in ascending order
- *in numerical order* – with the lowest coming first, i.e. in ascending order, or

with the highest coming first, i.e. in descending order

- *in date (or chronological) order.*

Validating

It is advisable to include some form of checking system so that the data which has been inputted is accurate. Sometimes, the level of accuracy is not as important as the bulk of the information itself, so the data-handling system will often have only a limited series of **validation** checks. In other cases, **check digits** may be used to make sure that data falls within the expected range. Although the computer may have a sub-system to carry out such validation checks, it is normally the responsibility of the operator to ensure that accurate data entry has been achieved. This normally means that the operator needs to visually check or proofread the information. Some organisations prefer to use a **double data entry system** where two operators input the same information so that cross-checking can be undertaken.

assignment

You must produce another report for the purpose of providing evidence for this element. Your report should incorporate all of the tasks given below:

task 1

Describe the methods of processing and types of data-handling system used in the organisation chosen by you during the previous element.

task 2

Again, using your chosen organisation, describe the objectives of its data-handling system.

task 3

Carrying on from the previous task, and still considering the objectives of the data-handling system you described, now state at least two data sources for that system.

task 4

Finally, your report should include at least one method of data capture for the data-handling system, and it should describe the processes applied to that data.

element

3.3

Use information technology for a data-handling activity

3.3.1

Identify database components, data types and keys required for a given data-handling activity

This element sets out the activities required for you to create a simple relational database. It is very closely related to Elements 3.1 and 3.2. Your teacher/tutor will be giving you several data-handling activities to explore.

In this performance criteria, we need to look in some detail at **databases** and the way they are used. In addition, we need to identify the different components which allow database software to function. Although the term database often implies that computers were the first to offer this function, the use of manual database systems has in fact been around for quite a long while. A telephone directory, where

the information provided is all of a similar kind and is placed in alphabetical order, is itself a form of database. Before computers made the job of storing information so much easier, quicker and more accurate, it was common to find the same or a similar kind of information being stored in card index boxes. Each card here would contain all the relevant information about one particular customer or supplier, and the cards would be filed in the box in alphabetical order. Let's look now at how a computer does exactly the same job, and identify the components which enable it to do this.

Database components

Fields

When we think about a telephone directory, we can see that all the information contained within it is 'related' since it is possible, with each entry in the directory, to obtain the following information:

- the name of the subscriber
- the address of the subscriber
- the postcode of the subscriber
- the area within which the subscriber lives
- the telephone number of the subscriber.

Each of these pieces of information is known as a **field**. Each field will be given a title, and it will then be necessary to estimate the amount of information one is likely to input into that field. For example, the name field will have to allow for company names as well as those of individuals. Having identified the title of the field and the length required, it will be necessary to identify what type of information will be inserted into this field. By type of information, we are concerned with that which the computer will recognise and be able to deal with. The following are field types:

- *text* – where the information contained in a telephone directory will be the name and address of the subscriber
- *number* – where the information contained in a telephone directory will be the postcode and telephone number of the subscriber.

It is also possible to create fields which accept the following types of information:

- surnames
- first names
- addresses
- postcodes
- dates of birth
- telephone numbers
- age.

The list is endless.

student activity

● COM 2.1, 2.2

How many other field names can you think of, and which different departments within an organisation would create and store this kind of database information? Write a list and compare your list to those of the remainder of your group.

Records

Having decided on the fields one will use within the database, it is now possible to start to create individual **records**, each of which will contain the same fields. Obviously, if some of the information is unavailable for one particular record, then the field will be left blank.

When creating the telephone directory, each of the subscribers will have their own record. All of the available information for each will be inserted into the relevant fields, and all the records together will form the telephone directory database. The information which is inputted into each field of a record is known as the **data**.

On the screen, when using a database program, only one record is shown at a time, though it is possible to view the 'list' of records. It is also possible to view a table to be designed. We look at this in the next section.

Tables

A **table** will be used to design the layout of

the database records. The layout can be amended at different stages of the design, and the table can be viewed either in its blank form or with some of the relevant information inserted. This will enable the user to see what the finished printed product will look like.

When deciding on the size of the fields to be included in the table, it is best to remember that the computer has only a limited amount of memory. For this reason, it is not advisable to make the fields too long since unnecessary space would waste the memory capacity. The ideal field length would allow just enough space for the data to be entered.

Relationships

Particularly when using a database to hold a lot of information about many hundreds of personnel, e.g. on personnel records held by a personnel department, it is often easier to have two or more files from each record which are 'related' to each other in some way. This will help to avoid the situation where one particularly large file is being used. We need to look at this in a little more detail:

- the personnel department of an organisation might wish to instruct its database to select specific fields from each of its staff records. This may be to find out how many employees are approaching their age of retirement
- because the information contained on each personnel record is related, it is possible to select only the date-of-birth field from each one
- the personnel department could then instruct the computer to select only those people with a date of birth occurring before a particular date and to print out only those records.

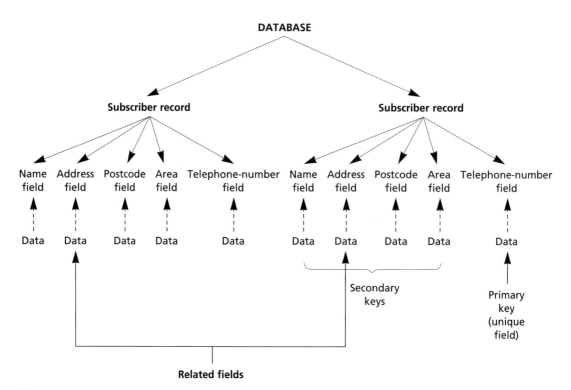

Figure 3.3.1 *Diagram of the database layout for a telephone directory*

If the records did not have related information, it would not be possible to instruct the computer to select in this way.

Data types

In the previous section, we looked at the two most commonly used types of field for individual records within a database, but now we need to consider the types of data which each field itself would contain. The following are the most common types of data:

- *text* – letters, numbers and symbols – i.e. **character** – can be entered into a **text field**, e.g. names and addresses. It is possible to sort this information into alphabetical and alphanumeric order
- *numbers* – it is possible to restrict the number of digits which can be inserted into a number field by removing any decimal points and rounding up to the nearest integer – i.e. whole number. This facility reduces the number of mistakes likely to be made because it limits the size of the numbers being inserted. It is possible to sort data into numerical order and to ask for information above ('>') or below ('<') a certain figure
- *dates* – it is possible to insert dates into a field so that searches for birthdays and diary entries can be made. This method will be used in our personnel-record example, by carrying out the search facility for those born before a certain date. A date format will be prepared as follows:

$$- -/- -/- -$$

so that the information will read, for example, as '01/01/97'.

- *time* – it is possible to insert data regarding the start and finish times of employees' working hours from information contained on their clocking-in and clocking-out cards. From this information, it can be calculated what overtime (if any) they have worked. In a similar way to the date format, time can be entered as:

$$- -/- -/- -$$

so that the information will read, for example, '08:30:45'.

Keys

In our telephone-directory example, there is one field which makes a record different from any other record. Obviously, this is the telephone-number field. Another term for this unique field, which distinguishes it and the total record from all the other fields in the database, is the **primary key**. Without this primary key, the computer will not be able to provide the search or select facility for us. A **secondary key** is also available. This is not unique like the primary key, but it can be used to allow different records to be grouped together. A good example of this in our telephone directory would be to link together all those people who live on a particular street or in a particular area of a town. Alternatively, the secondary key could be used to link together all those people who have the same surname.

3.3.2 Create a database

3.3.3 Enter and edit data

We have put these two performance criteria together because they are closely linked and equally practical in nature. In order to provide evidence for these two aspects of the unit, it will be necessary for you to undertake and successfully complete the element assignment given at the end of this section of the book. You have to prove that you can create a database by deciding what field names, types and lengths you will need. In addition, you then have to enter the relevant data and make amendments to it as necessary; this is known as **editing**.

As we have already learned when we discussed the editing of word-processed documents, editing means **amending** (changing), **appending** (adding) and **deleting** (taking out). If we use our telephone directory as the example here again, we see that it will have to be edited from time to time. The main reasons for this could include any of the following:

● someone's details might need to be amended because they have changed their name or address
● someone might need to be added as a new subscriber
● someone might need to be deleted because they no longer subscribe (possibly they have decided to be ex-directory).

Editing our telephone directory would be a very straightforward task. You would simply enter the primary key, i.e. the telephone number of the subscriber, and ask the computer to search for the relevant record, which would then appear on the screen. The relevant details for that subscriber could then be changed or deleted. If a new subscriber has to be added, then you would select the 'record' 'add' facility and a blank record would appear for you to complete. This would then be automatically filed in the correct alphabetical order.

3.3.4 Use facilities to generate database reports

The term 'generating a database report' means instructing a computer to search for a particular piece of information which you need. The report itself either will appear on the screen or can be printed onto hard copy. This can be done very quickly and easily, much more so than by using the manual method of searching through index cards. The computer will use a variety of ways to provide this report for you, and we shall now look at each in some detail.

Search using relational operators

When we discussed searching a database for those individuals who would reach retirement age this year, we talked about their date of birth being before a certain date. We have also mentioned 'more than' ('>') and 'less than' ('<'). This, in effect, involves the use of **relational operators** (as discussed in Element 2.3 on page 72) because we give the database instructions to limit its selection criterion to just one of the following options:

> something greater than a specified date
< something less than a specified date
= something equal to a specified date.

In the present example, the second option is selected.

Search using logic operators

The **logic operator symbols** are:

● and
● or
● not.

These are used because we want to include specific criteria and not others. When you use a logic operator to search a database, you use a different set of criteria from those involved with relational operators. Using the above example again, we could now ask for all those employees who are approaching retirement age and have been with the company for 'x' number of years. In this instance, you would input your relational operator but also include the term 'and' because you now have an additional criterion which has to be met. Similarly, a sports centre wishing to

identify those members who both swim and play bowls would also select the 'and' facility.

Selection of index key

All textbooks contain an **index** (usually at the end of the book) where you can identify the page number of the topic you wish to read. If a textbook did not contain this index, then it would take you a very long time to search through the book to find the information you require. Computerised databases use much the same method of indexing. They sort the different pieces of information into categories and file them away in order so that when you wish to obtain specific information, they can provide it. This is known as **indexing**.

Sort by selected key field

Sorting by selected key field means putting something into a certain order. You may ask the computer to produce a report in alphabetical or numerical order (which is the selected key field). It is possible to sort in more than one field. When we look at our telephone directory again, we can see that it is the case that more than one person has the same surname. In this case, the initials also go into alphabetical order, so for example:

● 'Brown, AJ' would appear before 'Brown, PD'
● 'Atkinson, SM' would appear before 'Atkinson, SP'.

When the telephone directory database is sorted into alphabetical order, the primary field will be the surname and then the initials will be considered.

assignment

In order to provide evidence for this element, it is necessary for you to produce a series of records which show that you have carried out the following:

- identified the different database components
- identified the different data types and keys for the data-handling activity
- created a database which includes at least two related tables
- correctly entered and edited the data contained in the database
- used the range of facilities available to you in order to generate database reports.

Your database could include the details of each member of your group, e.g. their names, addresses and telephone numbers. You could also include the number of people in their household. Alternatively, your database could include details of each person's employer, plus the latter's address and telephone number. Because several persons in your group will probably be employed by the same company, it will be necessary to create two related tables (files) to ensure that the company data is not repeated in a single person's table. If you use this method, you will need to identify the key which provides the relationship between tables, as well as the primary and secondary keys.

element

3.4

Examine safety and security issues

3.4.1 Apply accuracy checks to a data-handling activity

We have already discussed the importance of accuracy and the fact that no computerised system is efficient if the information inputted into it is inaccurate. All data-input operators need to be aware of the importance of accuracy, and to take certain steps to ensure that their work is error-free. Errors are reduced using computerised systems, but the information these systems produce is of course reliant upon the information they receive, and if this is inaccurate in the first place, then the computer cannot identify that inaccuracy on its own.

Validation

When we consider whether or not something is valid, we are asking whether it is suitable for its purpose, or whether it is

acknowledged by the computer as being of the correct type. In a database, we know that we have different field types, i.e. text or number. The computer will not accept data which is not of the right type (this is known as the **type check**), and this will reduce any data-input errors for the operator. In addition to this type-check **validation**, we have a **range check** facility, which limits a field by setting a particular range which it will accept. This range could be a minimum amount or a maximum amount, and if anything below or above this limit is entered, then the computer will not accept it. A good example here is that of a company which sells washing machines. If one of its retail outlets tries to order a washing machine at a particular price from the warehouse, then the range-check facility will come into operation. When the details of the washing

117

machine are inputted into the computer memory, the minimum amount it could be sold for would be entered (maybe £450) and a maximum amount may also be entered (maybe £510). When the retail-outlet assistant tries to request a machine to be sold at £445, this will not be accepted by the computer, and a message will appear on the assistant's screen indicating that this is outside the specified range. He/she will then have to re-enter the price being offered.

Verification

Verification is another word for checking. We already know that a word-processor operator will have to proofread and spellcheck documents before printing them to avoid the possibility of unnoticed errors being allowed to go out of the organisation. The spellcheck facility on computers is very efficient in most cases, but the operator still has to have a good knowledge of the English language as the computer cannot identify the misuse of certain words, such as 'weather' and 'whether'. In addition, the computer will accept the use of the words 'there' and 'their' but will not be able to identify whether or not they have been used in the correct context.

Proofreading may be very time-consuming. It is not always as easy to do when pages of numerical data are being keyed in, and it is sometimes necessary for other members of staff to check work. This may involve reading out the numbers or ticking down the page to ensure that all have been included.

When we discussed batch processing in this unit, we mentioned the fact that some organisations choose to have two members of staff keying in the same data so that errors can be avoided. This is another method of verification. The computer here will identify any discrepancies in the two sets of data and alert the operators to the errors that have been made.

Correctness

You may assume that **correctness** is the same as accuracy. This is not the case. Correctness means that the data which has been input into the computer has the correct meaning, whereas accurate means that the data is error-free. Correctness relates to the information which comes out of the computer. Useless information, even if it has been produced by the use of a computer, is still a waste of organisational time.

3.4.2

Apply security checks to a data-handling system

All organisations have to be security-conscious as all the information they hold, whether on computer or manually, is of use to their competitors. A sensible organisation will have a series of security

checks in operation in order to make sure that no important information is lost from its computer files. Although one would assume that the cost of losing its computer equipment would be of prime importance to an organisation, it is very often the case that it would be more costly and time-consuming if its *data* were lost, mainly because this may be irreplaceable or at least extremely difficult to replace.

Any such loss of data could occur in the following circumstances:

- a fire at the premises of the organisation
- the theft or corruption of data by employees or intruders
- accidental damage to data by employees who overwrite or delete files.

Organisations need to be particularly vigilant to ensure that no individual gains unauthorised access to either their premises or their computer systems. They must ensure that systems are in operation which restrict access to their data for the following reasons:

- confidential material could be held on computer systems which would be very useful to competitors or any person or organisation wishing to cause them some malicious damage
- the Data Protection Act of 1984 requires that organisations keep the information they hold regarding their employees, customers and suppliers in a secure manner.

Back-up

Obviously, any information which an organisation or an individual holds on a computer system should be backed up onto floppy disk or magnetic tape. The main advantage of this is that an exact replica of the data is made, and any unexpected problems with the hardware will not mean that important data is lost. It is easier and quicker to store small quantities of data onto disk, but more bulky data could be backed up on magnetic tape. Often, an organisation will

keep its back-up copies of files in fireproof containers in its archives or in an alternative building so that there is less likelihood of them being damaged as the result of a fire.

Confidentiality

Organisations will always have some information which will be classed as confidential because it could be of some use to their competitors. Employees are expected to adhere to the organisation's confidentiality rules. In fact, they may even have to sign a **confidentiality clause** in their contracts of employment. The breaking of this clause would result in their dismissal if they were found out to have been discussing or revealing confidential information about the organisation. The customers and suppliers of an organisation will also want to be assured that their information, which the organisation will have stored, is kept in a confidential manner.

Organisations will protect their confidential data by limiting its access to authorised personnel only and by ensuring that any wrongful access is highlighted immediately. One way of limiting access to such information is by use of **passwords**. This means that each individual will have a unique password which he/she has to key into the computer before it will allow him/her to gain access.

Obviously, all passwords will have to be kept confidential, in the same way that one would keep one's PIN number for one's bank or building society a secret. Such passwords will only allow the user certain levels of access to the data. More senior members of staff will probably have full access to any high-security data, whereas those in a more junior position will only be allowed into the less confidential and more routine material. It is also important that those users who are allowed access to the confidential material do not all have the option to make any changes to the data contained in the files: some should have 'read only'. An organisation will also need to be able to identify all those personnel who have accessed the files during the course of a given period. This is known as an **audit trail** of users.

Copyright

The Copyright, Designs and Patents Act 1988 protects individuals and organisations who have created material using a computer system. This legislation was designed to protect anyone creating the following either for themselves or on behalf of their organisation (if it was produced for the organisation by an employee, then it is the property of the business, not the individual):

- accounts materials
- all computer-produced documentation

- all computer-produced drawing (using CAD programs)
- all music written using a computer program
- any computer software.

The Act restricts anyone from doing any of the following:

- copying or changing any of the materials
- selling, renting or broadcasting the work
- misleading by stating that the work is your own.

Regular saving

We speak from experience when we tell you that it is vital to save information regularly, particularly if large amounts of data are being inputted. It only takes a power cut or a breakdown of some kind in the computer system for you to lose hours of work which has to be keyed in again. Do not rely on the automatic save facility on the computer!

3.4.3

Describe health and safety issues for information technology users

It is important that users of a computer be aware of the dangers of its use, and that users and employers alike take steps to avoid the problems we consider under the next three headings.

Stresses related to computer use

Eye strain

EU Directives are in force which specifically try to limit the occurrence of

eye strain for computer operators, and they state the following:

- that the screen of the computer should not reflect light, nor should it flicker, and that the brightness and contrast should be adjustable
- that the screen itself should be adjustable, to take into account the varying heights of the different users
- that no-glare screens should be used on the screens, and that a matt finish should be used on desks, keyboards and

surrounding walls the prevent the reflection of light

- that the overhead lighting should be suitable for computer users and should ensure a correct degree of contrast between the computer screen and the remainder of the room
- that all users of the computer screen should have the opportunity to take a free eye test at regular intervals throughout their working life.

Repetitive strain injury

Computer users and keyboard operators use the same repetitive movements on a day-long basis. They are constantly stretching the same muscles in their fingers and wrists in order to strike the keys, and this can cause the tendons to become swollen and painful. This ailment, **repetitive strain injury**, can result in an inability to carry out one's duties.

Bad posture whilst sitting at a computer can also result in back pain for users, and can also leave them unable to work for long periods of time.

Obviously, keyboard and computer operators should do all they can to try and avoid either of these problems occurring, including the following:

- making sure that they are sitting in the correct position. The keyboard should be adjustable and at the right angle
- making sure that their chair is capable of swivelling and is on castors so that they are not constantly putting pressure on their backs each time they need to change position. The chair should also have a back rest which can be adjusted to suit the height and posture of the user
- taking regular breaks from the screen in order to give the muscles a rest and to change posture
- making sure that the VDU (visual display unit) is at the correct distance from the eyes, and that the keyboard is

at the correct height for the posture of the user

- avoiding constant use of the computer by having a series of duties or tasks to perform every day which enable the user to walk away from the computer desk.

Radiation

In order to avoid the risk of radiation from the VDU, special screens can be fitted. Although the risk of radiation is said to be fairly minimal, there is a danger to pregnant women, who have suffered miscarriage as a direct result of using computers during their work activities. For this reason, it is unwise for pregnant women to spend lengthy amounts of time in front of VDUs.

Hazards

Costs of accidents and health problems

The cost of accidents and health problems related to work can be very high. Perhaps one of the easiest ways to measure this is in money terms. From the employer's point of view, the following costs may occur as a result of not making sure that accidents and health problems are avoided:

- having to pay for temporary staff to replace those employees who have fallen sick or have been injured at work
- the loss of work and disruption to other employees if one of their colleagues is off work
- the time and money that will have to be spent in training up staff to replace those who are off work
- the payment of welfare benefits to those who are off work

- the payment of compensation claims to those who have been injured or have fallen sick as a result of hazards and accidents in the workplace.

For the employee's part, there are also some costs to think about:

- even if the employee receives sickness benefit, this will not be as much as a regular wage
- if the employee is badly hurt or is permanently sick, then he/she may never return to work
- there are the costs of having to go to hospital, of clinics and of prescriptions.

There is no doubt that many accidents and hazards could be avoided if we all pay attention to the working environment in which we operate.

Before going on, let us now define three terms:

- a **danger** is the potential exposure to a hazard
- a **risk** is the chance of being hurt
- a **hazard** is a situation that may result in someone being injured or damaged.

student activity

● COM 2.1

Think about the following questions as a group.

- Can someone deliberately cause an accident?
- Do accidents normally mean that someone is injured?
- Do accidents usually mean damage to property?
- Do accidents normally mean damage to the environment?

Handling materials

There are a number of things to think about when you are using materials in the workplace. Obviously, the types of hazards and potential problems that might crop up will depend upon the sorts of materials that are used at the workplace. Here are some of the things that you should think about:

- materials should be stored in easily accessible places, particularly if they are heavy or bulky
- materials should be stored in dry and safe places
- materials that are not being used should be put away again as soon as possible
- materials should never be left in a place that would cause an obstruction to others
- materials should always be kept in containers which are designed for them and not others
- materials need to be disposed of if they become useless as they could become a hazard if they are left lying around.

Electricity guidelines

Probably the most important thing to think about when you are using machinery, tools or other equipment is the fact that they are powered by electricity. Some general safety points concerning this aspect are as follows:

- make sure that you always use the closest power point when plugging in a machine, tool or piece of equipment
- remember that trailing wires and flexes can cause accidents if they are left across areas that other people have to cross
- never overload an electrical socket when you could also use another one. It is very unwise to plug several pieces of equipment into the same socket using a multi-adaptor

- if you spot a broken socket or plug or a loose wire, never try to mend these yourself – report them to your supervisor or a technician
- when you have finished using a machine, tool or piece of equipment, always turn it off and unplug it. Make sure also that you always unplug it at the end of the day.

Handling machines, tools or equipment

Here are some general points to remember when using machines, tools and equipment:

- never try to use a machine, tool or piece of equipment for something that it is not designed for
- if there is anything wrong with the machine, tool or piece of equipment, never be tempted to try to mend it yourself. Switch it off, and then report the fault to someone – your supervisor or a technician
- if the machine is bulky and not meant to be moved, never try to move it. It has been placed there for a reason
- always read the manufacturer's and any other instructions related to the piece of equipment before you start to use it
- make sure that you can see what you are doing: never try to use machinery in poor light
- always use the protective equipment provided for the job. Never even turn on the machinery before you have put this protective equipment on
- make sure that you know the safety rules regarding the machinery before you attempt to use it
- never try to use a piece of equipment that you have been told not to touch or have never received any instructions or training about.

student activity

● **COM** 2.1

As a group, try to remember the times when you could have had an accident as a result of equipment. These could have been at home, at work or at the centre. Have any of you actually hurt yourself? What precautions would you take in the future?

Fire guidelines

Fire can be a constant concern in most workplaces. After all, we all use electrical equipment, and this is a major source of fire hazards. Here are some general things to think about in relation to fire (can you think of some reasons why these are good things to remember?):

- make sure that you know what the fire drills are, and that you practice evacuation at least once a year
- make sure that you read all of the fire notices that are displayed around the workplace
- make sure that you know where the fire equipment is and how to use it in an emergency
- make sure that the fire exits are always clear and not blocked at any time
- make sure that anything that could catch fire (i.e. that is **inflammable**) is stored away. Inflammable materials or objects must be kept out of direct sunlight as this may make them catch fire
- make sure that you do not smoke in areas that have been designated no-smoking areas. There may be very good reasons for this.

Health and safety equipment

Amongst the most common types of health and safety equipment, we will find the following:

- *personal protective equipment* – whenever toxic or otherwise dangerous materials or substances are present, protective clothing and equipment should be worn. It is always worth remembering that only the right sort of clothing should be worn since normal clothes can be caught in machinery too
- *ventilation* – good ventilation is essential in some workplaces as hazardous fumes and smoke are often created as a result of processes used. This is not a simple question of having windows open or doors kept ajar: extractor fans and machinery to circulate the air can be essential to ensure that sufficiently good air quality is maintained at all times
- *fire extinguishers* – there are a number of different fire-fighting pieces of equipment. These include the following:
  - water
  - carbon dioxide
  - powder
  - foam
  - halon

There are also fire blankets which are used to smother fires – particularly useful if someone is on fire. Buckets of sand are also used in the workplace

student activity

● **COM** 2.1

Referring to the above sorts of fire extinguisher, find out what each of the different types of material are used for. In what circumstances should you use certain types, and in what circumstances should you never use certain types?

Collect this information and compare it with the findings of the rest of your group.

- *safety warning signs* – these should always be clearly marked and put in places that can easily be seen by employees or by another person visiting the organisation. It should also be the case that the signs should never be covered or blocked from view for any reason. In addition to this, it may be necessary to put particular signs next to certain machines and equipment to make sure that the users understand the potential hazards that are associated with it

FIGURE 3.4.1 *Some examples of safety warning signs*

student activity

● **COM** 2.1

As a group, visit the various areas in your centre that have machinery or equipment and make a list of all of the safety warning signs that you can find. Are they all up-to-date and clearly visible? Make sure that you tell your tutor if you find any that are wrong.

● *first aid equipment* – some people in all organisations are trained to be first-aiders. These people should know how to deal with basic first-aid situations and be on hand to help if there is an accident. Under the Health and Safety at Work Act, an employer is required by law to make sure that qualified first-aiders are available. Normally, basic first-aid equipment is available in most organisations, and this will include the following items:
- bandages
- plasters
- splints
- an antiseptic
- safety pins.

student activity

● **COM** 2.1, 2.2

Can you think of other things that you would find in the first-aid box? What things should *not* be in there? How would you report the fact that certain items are missing, and who would have the responsibility to make sure that they are replaced? Write a list, compare your list with the rest of the group and then check with your tutor that you are correct.

EU and UK health and safety legislation

Although you are not expected to remember all of the rules and regulations that relate to health and safety in the workplace, always try to make sure that you do remember the main ones that relate to you and to the work that you are expected to carry out. In this way, you can help to ensure that neither yourself nor others are put in danger by your actions. Above all, if you see anything that could be considered a hazard, then it is your responsibility to make sure that a supervisor is made aware of it. You should also check that anything that you have noticed is put right as quickly as possible after you have reported it.

The following is a list of some points that you should always bear in mind when you are in the workplace:

- make sure that no gangways are blocked
- make sure that all fire exits are clear
- make sure that all fire doors are shut and never propped open
- make sure that you close filing-cabinet drawers after opening them: they can easily topple over and fall on someone
- make sure that all cigarettes are put out, and that you always observe the smoking rules of the organisation
- make sure that all electrical items are unplugged at the end of the day
- make sure that any adaptors or electrical wires are not trailing along the floor so as to cause someone to trip over them
- make sure that all faulty equipment is reported to the appropriate person immediately upon discovering the fault
- make sure that items are not stacked too high on shelves or in cupboards
- make sure that all frayed or damaged carpets are mended or covered until the repairs have been carried out
- make sure that all first-aid equipment is

in an accessible place and is always replenished after use

- make sure that unguarded fires are never used in the workplace
- make sure that all employees are familiar with the use of fire extinguishers, and that the fire drill is well-known throughout the organisation
- make sure that all valuable items are locked safely away at the end of the day.

All organisations are required to have a safety policy. They must make sure that they have done everything to avoid accidents and fires. This is normally achieved by the following steps:

- making sure that all employees receive a written safety policy
- making sure that all employees have a copy of the safety handbook
- making sure that the employees attend regular training sessions.

Health and Safety at Work Act

The Health and Safety at Work Act 1974, also known as HASAWA, sets out the responsibilities of employers and employees to ensure the following:

- that safe working practices are carried out in the workplace
- that the workplace is non-hazardous
- that the workplace is as healthy as possible.

The particular responsibilities of the employer are to ensure:

- that the workplace is kept as safe as possible
- that all of the equipment used in the workplace is safe and regularly serviced
- that any hazardous substances or materials are stored in such a way as to avoid potential danger

- that the employees have sufficient welfare facilities in the workplace
- that the workplace can be easily evacuated if a problem makes this necessary
- that they provide the employees with up-to-date and relevant training and supervision on a range of health and safety matters.

For the employees, HASAWA could not be clearer. Basically, they must take responsibility for their own area of work as well as for their own actions in the workplace. They should also immediately report any potential hazard to the employer or to a safety representative.

Before this act, employees were protected against hazardous working conditions under a number of different pieces of legislation. HASAWA aimed to bring all of these together and extend the protection of employees under a single act. The main points of HASAWA are as follows:

- it stated the general duties of an employer across all types of industry and commerce
- it created a system by which HASAWA could be enforced (by the Health and Safety Executive and local authorities)
- it created the Health and Safety Commission which aimed to help employers to understand the regulations and develop codes of practice
- it was backed up by the imposition of a series of legal obligations on the employer, who risked facing criminal proceedings for failure to follow them
- it imposed minimum safety regulations and introduced improvements to the working environment.

The work of HASAWA has been followed up by a number of EC Directives covering such areas as safety signs at work, employees handling hazardous materials and guidance regarding avoidance of major hazards.

New regulations and codes of practice are being designed continually and now cover nearly all work activities both in the private and the public sector. Steps are now being taken to cover any gaps in the legislation, or to make it easier to understand and implement.

Management of Health and Safety at Work Regulations

The Management of Health and Safety at Work Regulations 1992 is a major piece of legislation which aims to provide a systematic and well-organised set of guidelines in relation to health and safety. These include the following:

- employers are required to assess any potential risks employees may have to face and take preventive measures to cope with them
- this risk assessment must be continually monitored by a group of employers working closely with at least five employees
- employers are required to employ specialists whose sole responsibility it is to implement the preventive measures, as well as to provide information for all other employees within the organisation
- employers are further required to carry out regular screenings of their employees to make sure that they have not suffered any ill effects as a result of carrying out their duties. If appropriate, any health hazards which have been identified should be addressed immediately
- employees who have been given the duties of safety representatives should be regularly consulted, provided with time and space to carry out their investigations and given the authority to act on them.

Health and Safety (Display Screen Equipment) Regulations

The Health and Safety (Display Screen Equipment) Regulations 1992 are designed to protect employees who spend considerable amounts of their working hours in front of a computer screen. The main points of the legislation are as follows:

- employees must receive sufficient breaks from the screen
- the work should not be repetitive, and the employee should be given a variety of tasks
- basic safety requirements must be satisfied as regards the screen itself and the design of the keyboard, as well as the shape and height of the desk and chair being used
- regular eye tests must be provided by the employer, and if the employee needs special spectacles in order to carry out his/her tasks, these should be provided by the employer
- efficient lighting should be provided in the room where the employee is using the computer, as should proper ventilation.

Factories Act

The Factories Act 1961 covers a wide range of different organisations, focusing on the use of machinery. The key features of this piece of legislation are as follows:

- the employer must provide toilet and washing facilities
- premises should be adequately heated and ventilated
- the employer must make sure that floors, stairs and passageways are not obstructed in any way
- all floors should have a non-slippery surface
- potentially dangerous machinery should be fenced off to protect employees

FIGURE 3.4.2 *The British Safety Council leaflet for computer users*

- the employer must ensure that there are adequate fire escapes, well signposted and regularly maintained
- fire doors should never be locked or obstructed.

Offices, Shops and Railways Premises Act

The Offices, Shops and Railways Premises Act 1963 concentrates on conditions within shops and offices and provides a number of clear guidelines to the employer, including the following:

- in work areas, the temperature must never drop below 16 °C
- the employer must ensure that there is an adequate supply of fresh air
- following on from the Factories Act 1961, this legislation states that the employer must provide enough toilet

and washing facilities in relation to the number of staff. He/she must also make sure that there is hot and cold running water, as well as soap and clean towels

- again, following on from the Factories Act 1961, this legislation states that an employer has to provide suitable lighting wherever employees are expected to work or move around
- the employer must ensure that there is at least 12 square metres of working space per employee.

Consumer Protection Act

There are countless cases of people being injured by defective products, and they may have the right to sue for damages. The term **product liability** is given to those laws that govern these rights. In the past, an injured person had to prove that the manufacturer was negligent, but under the Consumer Protection Act of 1987, an injured person can now sue a supplier without having to prove negligence under the sale-of-goods law. It is also worth remembering the fact that this also applies to individuals who have been injured whether or not they have had the product sold to them.

When a person is injured, action can be taken against one (or more) of the following:

- the producers or manufacturers of the product
- the importers of the product (strictly speaking, the importers of the product into the EC)
- the suppliers of own-brand products
- wholesalers and retailers that do not disclose the true producer of the product.

Liability under the Consumer Protection Act is not just restricted to consumer products. With the exception of unprocessed agricultural products and

buildings, all other products are also covered (including those used at work). With regard to buildings, the materials used are covered (i.e. the bricks, cement and wood etc.).

A **defective product** is strictly defined as one where the safety of that product is not as the person who is using it should expect. A product is not defective just because it is of poor quality, and it is not defective if there is a safer version on the market.

When looking at a defective product, the court will consider the following:

- the way in which the product is marketed
- any instructions (or warnings) that might be given
- what the product should be reasonably used for
- the time that the producer supplied the product.

Warnings and instructions should be made clear particularly in cases when it is known that the product is misused. A good example of this would be **solvents**.

An injured person can sue under the Consumer Protection Act for **compensation**:

- if the product has resulted in a death
- if the product has resulted in injury
- if the damage has resulted in the loss of property valued at more than £275.

It still remains the responsibility of the injured person (or **plaintiff**) to show that it is the defect in the product that has caused the damage.

The producer or importer can attempt to avoid the liability of an alleged defective product by proving one of the following:

- that he/she did not actually supply the product in question (perhaps it was stolen or is a copy of his/her product)
- that the scientific and technical knowledge at the time the product was

supplied did not suggest that the product was defective.

- that the defect was a result of having to comply with the law. The producer/supplier will need to show here that the law had the unavoidable effect of making the product defective.
- that the defect came about after the product had been supplied (for example, the retailer may not have taken reasonable steps to prevent damage or defects from occurring)
- that the supplier is not actually a business. This instance includes products that are made at home, products not for resale or second-hand goods
- that the defect occurred as a result of a defective component made by another producer.

In all cases, the plaintiff must begin the court action within three years of being injured by the defective product. The injured person cannot sue under the Act three years after the defective product was supplied by the producer (as, for example, with old stock in a retail outlet).

3.4.4

Describe the obligations of users of information technology

Rights of the individual

The Data Protection Act 1984 has had enormous implications for all organisations which have access to or store information about their customers and employees. As you will see from the list below, an individual about whom an organisation has information stored, does have specific rights, and these include:

- the right of access to that information
- the right to challenge inaccurate information.

If an organisation fails to comply with the Data Protection Act in this respect, then the individual affected has a right to be compensated.

There are some exceptions to this, however. These are:

- where the individual has supplied the information him/herself

- where the organisation has taken 'all reasonable care' to acquire the information
- where the information relates to payroll matters
- where the information relates to pension details
- where the information is used only for statistical purposes, and in addition does not specifically identify any individuals.

Lawful use of data

The Data Protection Act attempts to ensure that stored information is only put to specific lawful purposes. Whilst it is difficult to maintain this degree of certainty about the usership of the information, most organisations will tend to use stored information for its specifically stated purpose only. Problems will inevitably arise, however, when this information is exchanged between different organisations. The organisation which initially collected the data may have had one specific purpose in mind, whereas the organisation which has acquired the information may have different motives altogether. The transmission of sensitive information from one organisation to another can pose considerable problems both to individuals and to the Data Protection Registrar. In particular, information stored regarding an individual's creditworthiness may include a number of inaccuracies which have not been identified. If the individual subsequently discovers such inaccuracies, then it is a difficult task to trace the transmission and use of the original inaccurate information in order to ensure that all the relevant information stored at whatever location is, indeed, accurate.

The Data Protection Act makes it a legal requirement that an organisation take steps to ensure that unauthorised access is avoided, and a breach of security in this respect can mean fines for the organisation in question. The sensitivity of some material stored is such that it could be used for criminal or other unlawful purposes by an unauthorised entrant. This sensitivity factor is further heightened by the fact that the individual whose information is stored in the system may be unaware that it is there. If unauthorised entry is gained and this information is used by others, then the individual may suffer as a result.

Most organisations keep detailed records which may include the following:

- customers' names and addresses
- customer transactions
- customer credit information
- specific information regarding customers, such as their political affiliations (in recent years, certain high-street banks have admitted that they keep details of customers' political allegiances)
- staff records
- personal information regarding employees' domestic situations

- disciplinary action taken against employees.

The Data Protection Act requires all organisations or individuals who hold personal details regarding other individuals on computer to register with the Data Protection Registrar. If an organisation or individual fails to do this, then they may be fined up to £2,000. The Registrar needs to know the following:

- what sort of information is held
- what use is made of the information
- who else has access to this information
- what methods were used to collect the information.

The Registrar must ensure that the data conforms with the Act. Specifically, this means that the Registrar must ensure that:

- the information has been collected in an open and fair manner
- the information is only held for lawful purposes
- the uses to which the information is put are disclosed to the Registrar
- the information held is relevant to the purpose for which it is held
- the information is accurate
- the information is up-to-date
- any irrelevant or inaccurate information is destroyed
- individuals can be told about the existence of the information
- individuals can challenge inaccurate information
- the information is kept confidential
- the organisation takes steps to ensure that unauthorised access is avoided.

student activity

● **COM** 2.1, 2.2

Consider, from a personal point of view, the Data Protection Act and try to assess the range and amount of information about you which may be stored by organisations. Write a list of any considerations you can think of, and then compare your list to those of the remainder of your group. How much do they vary?

Accuracy of data

The fifth principle of the Data Protection Act states that 'personal data shall be accurate and, where necessary, kept up to date'. The Act gives further guidance on interpreting this principle. 'Accurate' means correct and not misleading as to any matter of fact. A mere opinion, which does not purport to be a statement of fact, cannot be challenged on the grounds of inaccuracy.

The Act contains special provisions which apply to information obtained either from the data subject him/herself or from third parties. Stated briefly, a data user who wishes to rely on these provisions must ensure that both the fact that the information has come from such a source, and any challenge by the data subject to the accuracy of the information are recorded. If these requirements are complied with, the fact that the personal data is inaccurate does not result in a breach of the above-mentioned principle.

The Registrar will seek to establish that there is a factual inaccuracy and will also wish to see whether the data user has taken all responsible steps to prevent it. The matters which he/she may wish to consider will include:

● the degree of significance of the inaccuracy
● the source from which the inaccurate information was obtained
● any steps taken to verify the information
● the procedures for data entry and for ensuring that the system itself does not introduce inaccuracies into the data
● the procedures followed by the data user when the inaccuracy came to light.

If an individual suffers damage because of inaccurate personal data held about him/her by a data user, he/she is entitled to claim compensation from that user. An application for compensation must be made by the individual to the court: compensation cannot be awarded by the Registrar.

Data protection and use of equipment

In order to decide whether or not the Data Protection Act affects the activities of an organisation, it will have to be considered whether the organisation uses any of the following:

● word processors
● micro-computers
● minicomputers
● mainframe computers.

In making this decision, the organisation should remember that it makes no difference whether the equipment is owned or leased. It is not the equipment itself that is important, but the use of that equipment for the storage and processing of data. If any of the above are used by an organisation, then the following questions need to be addressed about the equipment:

● is it used for the processing of accounts payable and accounts received?

- is it used for the checking of credit ratings?
- is it used for the payroll and for the storage of personnel data?
- is it used for marketing and sales information?
- is it used for the storage of general management information?
- is it used for the production and manipulation of letters and text?
- is it used for the transmission of electronic mail?

If the organisation does use its equipment for any of the above, then these activities need not be considered for restriction by the legislation.

On the other hand, if an organisation can identify that it stores and uses *personal data* and has to ensure that this is properly secured, then this does require special attention. The data-protection laws frequently refer to specific types of personal data which are either prohibited or must have special safeguards, as detailed earlier. This data relates to:

- racial origin
- political opinions
- religious beliefs
- health.

If it uses a **computer service bureau**, an organisation is not responsible for ensuring that personal data is processed only in a properly controlled environment. Here, the computer service bureau instead has to register that it provides processing services to other organisations and must conform to the requirements laid down for security and confidentiality.

If an organisation's computer system holds any data regarding the following, then it must ensure that it is conforming to specific domestic legislation:

- the sexual life of employees
- any criminal convictions of employees
- the colour of skin of employees

- the use of intoxicants by employees
- the intimacy of the private life of its employees
- the trade union membership or otherwise of its employees.

Consent to disclosure

The personal data held by the data user may include information which identifies another individual as well as the data subject, e.g. a relative or associate of the data subject or a person who has given information to the data user about the data subject. In replying to a request from the data-subject, the data user need not disclose the information about the other individual unless that other individual has consented to a disclosure. However, the data user must still give as much information as possible to the data subject without revealing the other individual's identity. This may involve editing the information to remove names or other identifying details. Information should not be withheld under this provision merely because the data user suspects that the data subject may be able to guess the other individual's identity. The provision applies only where anyone lacking the data subject's special knowledge could reasonably be expected to identify the other individual from the information.

The fact that another individual's consent may be required should never prevent the data user from replying at least partially to the request. When he/she has received the request, together with enough information about identity and location, the data user should in fact always reply within 40 days, and the reply should consist of:

- confirmation that personal data about that individual is held
- a copy of as much of the information as can be given without disclosing the identity of the other individual who has not consented.

student activity

● **COM** 2.2, 2.4
● **IT** 2.1, 2.2, 2.3

There are several exemptions and restrictions set down in the guidelines relating to the Data Protection Act. Obtain a copy of these leaflets and research the following:

● what data is exempt from the regulations?
● what disclosures are prohibited by law?
● how likely is it that data relating to one individual could be accessed and purchased by another individual or organisation?

Present your findings in the form of a word-processed report.

Costs of implementing the Act

Obviously, one of the negative effects of the implementation of the Data Protection Act for an organisation could be the costs involved. If the organisation is large and the amount of information stored is of a nature to require registration with the Registrar, then some expense will be involved in overseeing the input of such data. It may be necessary for the organisation to employ an individual to control and monitor this process. Such a Data Protection Officer will have responsibility for monitoring the addition, deletion and use of information. This could involve a great deal of time in man hours and expense in terms of salaries for the organisation.

student activity

● **COM** 2.1, 2.4

Again, as in the previous activity, obtain copies of the guidelines regarding the implementation of the Data Protection Act. You will find that your college or local library will have copies. Try to estimate the cost to an organisation of complying with the legislation. Does it cost more for an organisation than it does for an individual? Discuss your findings with the remainder of your group.

Theft

Apart from the physical removal of equipment and software, there are a number of cases where computer fraud can be committed in order to make some kind of financial gain. Some of the most common forms of computer fraud include:

● entering incorrect additional or unauthorised data. This can also include modifying data or installing a system which does not allow other data from other users to be installed
● destroying or altering outputs such as print-outs or summaries so that any fraud continues to remain unnoticed
● altering files in order to transfer cash or to amend an individual's personal record
● using **patching programs** which trigger a sub-routine to channel funds into a bogus account
● creating a **suspense account** which again diverts funds into a bogus personal account.

An organisation which uses computers will

be best advised to take the following measures:

- restrict access to computer hardware
- regularly audit data
- regularly change procedures
- regularly change passwords and **entrance protocol**
- regularly monitor programming.

Virus checking

A **computer virus** is a program which either aims to cause a nuisance to the unsuspecting user or has a rather more sinister and serious intent. Viruses can be 'caught' by a computer simply by the use of a disk which has not been scanned for hidden or unexplained files. Once such a disk has been used, the program will transfer itself into the computer's main memory and may often hide itself in the boot sector. From here, it can infect all other media which are used on the computer, which has serious implications if the computer is networked or has some form of connection with other computers.

Viruses can be best avoided if all users take the following steps:

- ensure that only **first generation** or original disks are used when installing software
- ensure that **write-protect** disks are used for reading purposes
- ensure that up-to-date virus-checking and detection software is used at regular intervals
- ensure that the majority of workstations do not have disk drives
- ensure that only authorised software is installed or run on the organisation's main computer systems.

EU and UK copyright legislation

Computer software is now covered under the Copyright, Designs and Patents Act 1988, although there are moves to fall in line with European legislation which extends copyright from 50 years to 70 years after the death of the author or creator.

Copyright applies to all work, whether it is published or not, and for information-technology purposes, such work is the software that has been developed by, and used only by, a single organisation. In its simplest form, copyright is indicated by the symbol '©' plus the name of the copyright owner(s) and the date of first publication. On other software or related materials, there may also be the phrase 'all rights reserved'. In other cases, this is even more firmly put by the use of the phrase 'no part of this publication may be reproduced or transmitted in any form or by any means without permission'.

In information-technology terms, copyright legislation is intended to cover the following areas:

- the pirating of copyright-protected software
- copying pirated software into the memory of a computer
- transmitting software through telecommunications.

The question of copyright and the problems associated with it are so serious that the major software publishers have founded the Federation Against Software Theft, which was the prime mover in getting computer software included in the Copyright, Designs and Patents Act 1988.

assignment

For the first two performance criteria of this element, your tutor will observe you carrying out accuracy and security checks whilst handling data. For the remainder of this element you will be expected to give a presentation which covers the two remaining performance criteria.

task 1

Describe the various health and safety issues for users of information technology.

task 2

Describe the obligations of users of information technology.

End test questions

1 Which TWO of the following are industrial organisations?

   1   a car manufacturer
   2   a fire station
   3   a frozen food processor
   4   a job centre.

     a   1 and 2
     b   2 and 3
     c   3 and 4
     d   1 and 3.

2 Which ONE of the following departments is responsible for obtaining orders for its products from customers?

   a   accounts
   b   personnel
   c   sales
   d   production.

3 Which ONE of the following departments is responsible for recruitment of new staff?

   a   accounts
   b   personnel
   c   sales
   d   production.

4 Which ONE of the following would be regarded as an internal function of an organisation?

   a   interviewing a candidate for a post
   b   holding a health and safety meeting
   c   advertising
   d   holding a sales convention.

5 Which ONE of the following documents would be received with an order?

   a   an order form
   b   an invoice
   c   a delivery note
   d   a credit note.

6 Which ONE of the following would be received by an organisation as a request for payment for goods sent to them by a supplier?

   a   an order form
   b   a delivery note
   c   a statement of account
   d   a credit note.

7 Which ONE of the following documents would be sent to request payment from a customer?

a   an order form
b   a delivery note
c   a statement of account
d   a credit note.

8 Which ONE of the following would be sent to a supplier requesting goods?

a   an order form
b   a delivery note
c   a statement of account
d   a credit note.

9 Which TWO of the following are likely to be produced using transaction processing?

1   a letter responding to a complaint from a customer
2   an electricity bill which is sent out quarterly
3   a till receipt
4   an annual optician appointment.
  a   1 and 2
  b   2 and 3
  c   3 and 4
  d   1 and 4.

10 Which ONE of the following is likely to be produced using batch processing?

1   a letter responding to a complaint from a customer
2   an electricity bill which is sent out quarterly
3   a till receipt
4   an annual optician appointment.

11 Which TWO of the following are likely to be benefits of a computerised stock control system?

1   recording the cost of all products in stock
2   alerting the organisation to serious overstocking

3   increasing the sales
4   increasing the storage space.
  a   1 and 2
  b   2 and 3
  c   3 and 4
  d   1 and 4.

12 Which TWO of the following are methods of data capture?

1   a visual display unit
2   a bar code reader
3   a magnetic reader
4   a printer.
  a   1 and 2
  b   2 and 3
  c   3 and 4
  d   1 and 4.

13 Which ONE of the following would be the most suitable data source for a research project on foreign currency?

a   a bar code
b   a first aid manual
c   Prestel
d   scanner.

14 Which ONE of the following would be the most suitable data source for a research project on staff qualifications?

a   a bar code
b   Prestel
c   scanner
d   personnel files.

15 If a database was required to be produced in ascending alphabetical order, which ONE of the following would be used to produce this?

a   selecting
b   sorting
c   calculating
d   validating.

16 If, from a database, only those records which relate to certain criteria are required, which ONE of the following would be used to produce this?

a selecting
b sorting
c calculating
d validating.

17 If an organisation wishes to pay its staff a 10 per cent Christmas bonus, provided they have been with the organisation from 2 years or more, which TWO of the following processes would be used?

1 selecting
2 sorting
3 calculating
4 validating.
    a 1 and 2
    b 2 and 3
    c 3 and 4
    d 1 and 3.

18 An organisation keeps the following information in its personnel records about each individual member of staff: name, address, department, telephone extension number. The information for each of the individuals is stored as:

a a file
b a field
c a record
d a table.

Questions 19 and 20 are related to Text 1.

Text 1

The diagram below is a section from a database. You should answer the questions below:

A → Name   S Kemp
B → Job title   Accounts Clerk
C → Salary   £12,000
D → Personnel number   SK41175

19 Which ONE of the fields is likely to be a numeric format?

a A
b B
c C
d D.

20 Which ONE of the following is likely to be the primary key for this record?

a A
b B
c C
d D.

21 Which TWO of the following would be required in order to extract from a database the number of employees who have GCSE in English?

1 a search using relational operators
2 a search using logical operators
3 a selection by single index key
4 a sort by a single selected key field.
    a 1 and 2
    b 2 and 3
    c 3 and 4
    d 1 and 4.

22 What is the MAIN purpose of a range check?

a to allow verification
b to allow validation
c to allow type check
d to allow disclosure.

23 What is the MAIN purpose of a spellcheck facility?

a to allow verification
b to allow validation
c to allow type check
d to allow proofreading.

24 Which TWO of the following could be considered as health stresses related to computer use?

1 eye strain

2   repetitive strain injury
3   tiredness
4   sickness.
    a   1 and 2
    b   2 and 3
    c   3 and 4
    d   1 and 4.

25 The Health and Safety (Display Screen Equipment) Regulations 1992 state that employees must receive sufficient breaks from the screen. This is to ensure that:

  a   employees do not get bored
  b   to reduce radiation from the screen
  c   to prevent them making too many mistakes
  d   to give everyone a chance at the machine.

26 The Health and Safety At Work Act (1974) aims to:

  a   have all accidents reported
  b   reduce radiation from the screen
  c   ensure a responsible attitude to safety
  d   ensure data is kept securely.

27 In order to decide whether or not the Data Protection Act affects the activities of an organisation, it will have to be considered whether the organisation uses which TWO of the following:

1   word processors
2   mainframe computers
3   switchboards
4   photocopying machines.
    a   1 and 2
    b   2 and 3
    c   3 and 4
    d   1 and 4.

28 Disclosure of information covered by the Data Protection Act is restricted to:

  a   the individual concerned
  b   anyone requesting the information
  c   anyone requesting the information provided they have a letter
  d   relatives or friends of the individual concerned.

29 A computer virus can be best avoided by taking which ONE of the following steps?

  a   ensuring that only first generation or original disks are used when installing software
  b   ensuring that only one person ever uses the computer
  c   ensuring that passwords and entrance protocol are regularly changed
  d   ensuring that data is regularly audited.

30 EU and UK copyright legislation intends to cover which ONE of the following areas?

  a   the pirating of copyright-protected software
  b   the playing of computer games on computers
  c   the playing of computer games on CD-ROM
  d   the playing of computer games on video recorders.

element

4.1

Describe electronic communication systems and computer networks

Electronic communications are an important part of information technology. They allow organisations to send and receive information to and from remote locations. Typically, electronic communication systems will include telephones, radios, televisions, facsimile machines and computer systems. In this section, we will investigate the various electronic communication systems and networks and identify their key characteristics.

4.1.1 Describe and give electronic communication systems

Organisations need to be able to communicate with one another across the globe. There have been considerable developments in communication in this century which would have been unthinkable in the past. The instant transfer of complex information is now commonplace, coupled with the ability of any individual, correctly connected to a network, to be able to access information from anywhere in the world. Obviously, computer networks provide the basis for most of this advanced technology. However, we will also need to consider some of the more commonplace broadcast systems which facilitate information transfer.

Broadcast systems

Whenever a television or radio studio broadcasts a programme, the signal is carried to a receiver or series of receivers through a network of **transmitters**. These transmissions are either **VHF** (**very high frequency**) or **UHF** (**ultra high frequency**). Recent developments have also allowed broadcasts to be made via cable connections or **communication satellites**. Television broadcasting, for example, incorporates the ability to transmit sound, data and moving pictures on one-way basis. As an integral part of this, television broadcasters are also able to transmit network services such as Teletext or Ceefax, but this does mean that the television receiver needs to have a **decoder** to access this service.

Teletext and Ceefax are also known as Videotext, and this service is based on a central computer database which may contain many thousands of pages of information that can be regularly updated. Viewdata is very similar in appearance to Teletext or Ceefax, and also allows remote sites to receive information from a central database via a menu system. Typically, this latter service will provide information to travel agents or turf accountants, giving updated information on flight or holiday availability or on the results of a horse race. Users of these services will require a **modem** to receive this **digitised** or **analogue** data, which involves some investment in hardware and software.

Microwaves are also known as **SHF** (**super high frequency**). Broadcasters can bounce these waves against communication satellites, and they can then be picked up by another ground-based station. This station can then bounce the waves back to another satellite in order to increase the range of the broadcast. Satellite communication is becoming much more common, and not only are there a bewildering number of television stations that broadcast in this manner, but businesses will also use them for inter-site communications.

Another development arising out of the

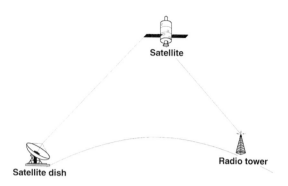

FIGURE 4.1.1 *SHF (super high frequency) waves passing from one broadcasting station to another by being bounced off a satellite*

gradual availability of cable services in the UK is the linking of sites over a wide area to receive satellite and terrestrial broadcasts as well as telephone services. Subscribers can also access videos on demand from an immense library of films and programmes, though this is only in pilot form in some areas.

Cellular radio communications operate in the UHF band. A number of base stations, positioned at strategic points around the countryside, allow each cell phone to access the network. These signals can penetrate most barriers, and for the most part, the spread of coverage is complete, except in areas of difficult terrain. Computers are used to maintain the links between the cell phone and the base stations, even whilst the user is moving. Obviously, this involves transferring from one base station to another if the user is making a call for a period of time whilst moving fast along a motorway. (There are very brief interruptions to the call whilst this transfer is made). Each base station can be considered to be a cell, and in cities these cells are very small, whilst in rural areas they are much larger. Each phone within a cell uses a different frequency so that the call cannot be interrupted or listened into by an unauthorised individual. Obviously, given the technology related to cellular phones, the user can not only transmit voice messages but also download or receive data which can then be loaded onto his/her own computer.

At one stage in the 1970s, Citizen Band (CB) Radio was an extremely popular way of facilitating two-way short-distance communication. Although in recent years it has lost favour to the more technologically advanced cellular phones, it still has a considerable following. CB is still used by the police and marine and aircraft control as a primary means of communication.

Telephones

Telephone communication has expanded beyond its original use as a means of connecting individuals who wish to talk to one another. It is now common practice for digital data to be sent through telephone systems, which has greatly increased the use of telephones as a primary electronic communication network. Other developments include **video phones** which allow users both to talk to and to see one another.

Facsimile machines

Facsimile machines are extremely common in most business organisations and also allow users to send documents via the telephone network. The fax machine at the sender's end converts the document into an electronic form and transmits it via the telephone line. The receiver's fax machine then converts it back into an exact copy of the original.

The obvious development in fax-based technology has been to do away with the need to produce an original hard copy of a

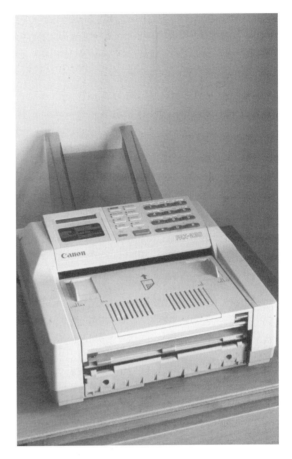

FIGURE 4.1.2 *A fax machine*

document. Computers are now able to 'fax' a document direct from the screen via a modem to the receiver, and this operates in exactly the same way as any other communication transmitted electronically by a computer. At the receiver's end, the choice can then be made as to whether the receiver wishes to print out a hard copy of the document or simply refer to it on screen.

Networks

As you already know, a stand-alone system comprises one screen or VDU, one keyboard and mouse, and possibly two disk drives: the hard drive and the floppy-disk drive. It may be, however, that an organisation has decided to **network** its computers.

Local area networks

A **local area network (LAN)** of micro-computers is a facility which allows users to be able to share information. When an employee who is working on a computer network system updates some information, another employee working at a different station on the same network can also inspect this information. This sort of system is particularly useful to organisations who have several people working on the same information at the same time. In addition, it allows the management of an organisation to retrieve information from the system without having to disturb their employees in doing so. The number of computers which can be linked to such a network is not restricted and can be increased or decreased as required.

Multi-user networks

Multi-user networks are very similar to networking micro-computers except that the system here involves just one computer which has a number of **terminals** attached to it. Each of the terminals is not a computer in its own right, and this gives the benefit of easier **booting up**. Obviously, if an organisation decides to network its computer system, then appropriate and compatible software will have to be acquired.

Public wide area networks

Public wide area networks are accessible to most of the public. These are generally telephone and cable TV networks which are wired up to many different homes. They usually include the **public switched**

telephone network and the **integrated digital services network**. The Internet is the most widely available version of this type of network, and this allows users to connect their personal computer to any number of other computers or mainframes in the world which hold a database or compatible electronic communication system.

Private wide area networks

Private wide area networks use privately leased or owned lines and do not offer the general public connection facilities. These private **WANS** may provide network services to subscribers, and offer facilities to enable access through **gateways** to other networks. Typically, these include cash-point machines (also known as **automatic teller machines**), **electronic point-of-sale (EPOS) terminals** and cable television. In all cases, access to these private wide area networks is restricted to authorised users or subscribers.

Benefits of computer networks

As we will see when we consider the types of service available on networks and their relative benefits, the main advantage of computer networks is the sharing of hardware, software and data. In addition to this, there are considerable advantages in being able both to control access to information and services and to provide a viable framework which enables individuals in remote locations to operate as part of a team.

Central services

Most organisations which have a computer network will delegate the responsibility for security and software to a **network manager**. This individual will determine which of the users will have access to particular services and data held on the network. He/she will also be responsible for ensuring that data-protection laws are adhered to and that there is no copyright infringement. One of the principal duties of a network manager will also be the regular and systematic backing up of files to ensure that vital information is not lost as a result of computer errors or accidents. On a regular basis, he/she will also delete unnecessary files in order to ensure that the network is not cluttered with information and that there is sufficient space available on the network to load and store new data. In carrying out all of these duties, the network manager ensures that the network is running smoothly and that the considerable benefits of networking all of the computers is enjoyed by the business.

In consultation with individuals in the organisation, the network manager will also ensure that all required software is available to be accessed by named users, and that any appropriate site payments have been made to the owners of the software.

Shared resources

Given the complexities of the majority of modern software applications, many stand-alone PCs are not sufficiently powerful to cope with all of the demands that may be placed upon them. A network allows an organisation to load software and store data in one central location which can be accessed by a number of different users. It is less expensive to store the application once rather than to have to store it a number of times on different machines. In addition to this, having one such central location means that new versions of software can be installed for immediate access by all users, rather than updated disks having to be distributed to a variety of different stand-alone computers.

Teamworking

As we have already mentioned, the use of a network enables individuals in a number of remote locations to work closely with one another and share resources, experiences and abilities. In this way, the relative strengths of each of the team members can be better employed by the organisation in order to compete tasks in a much more efficient way than would be the case with a number of individuals working independently.

Types of network service

Most modern organisations no longer operate from a single site. Even if they do, the position of various individuals within that organisation does not necessarily relate to, or assist, normal work patterns which involve operating with other individuals in different departments. For this reason, organisations will incorporate a number of essential network services within their systems to allow individuals to communicate with one another and gain access to centrally-held data and resources.

Bulletin boards

Bulletin boards operate rather like a noticeboard, allowing individuals to leave messages which can be read by others who access the service. Various information, such as notices or memoranda to all staff, can be found on an internal bulletin board, or a bulletin board may be set up by a service or product provider to keep users or purchasers informed of new developments. On the Internet, there are numerous bulletin boards, either free or requiring a subscription, which hold some very useful information which can be accessed and downloaded by any user.

Conferencing

In its most primitive form, **conferencing** allows a number of individuals to speak to one another simultaneously over a telephone network. In the last few years, **video-conferencing** has also become available, allowing both an audio and a visual link-up. At present, the cost of setting up a video-conferencing centre is so high that organisations tend to use services provided by other businesses which have the appropriate studio facilities. New developments have also allowed conferencing to take place via a network of computers, with either a full screen or a window image of those involved in the conversation being displayed. The principal advantage of video-conferencing is that it enjoys many of the benefits of face-to-face communication. Typically, a computer-based conferencing system requires each terminal to have a camera and microphone connected, as well as the appropriate software to handle the transmissions of audio and visual images.

Electronic mail

Electronic mail (**email**) offers all of the facilities provided by fax and telex but is paperless. Electronic mail offers the additional advantage of being able to store messages even when the destination terminal is busy.

Electronic mail systems offer a variety of common features, including:

- terminals to prepare and store messages
- a communication link with other workstations within the network
- a central controlling computer
- a directory of addresses
- a central mailbox
- a system which dates the messages
- a function that notes that a message has been received by the addressee
- a facility to multiple-address, so that all members of a particular working group can be sent a message simultaneously
- a prioritising system, so that messages can be identified as either important or routine
- a storage facility in order to keep, in the memory, those messages that have not yet been received
- compatibility with existing equipment and computer systems.

Electronic mail offers a number of advantages in relation to other forms of communication, including:

- savings on stationery and paper costs
- savings on telephone costs
- rapid transmission
- integration with other systems
- the recording of all transmissions so that accurate costings can be obtained
- allowing employees to **telework**
- allowing addressees to peruse their own electronic mail at their leisure.

Another version of the electronic-mail system may be found in the Electronic Data Interchange, which enables individuals to exchange business documents using the same communication system. Electronic diaries and calendars are becoming increasingly common and allow individuals to make diary entries and searches on particular days or events, thus avoiding the need to enter information manually into a personal handwritten business diary.

File transfer

File transfer simply refers to the facility which enables a user to transfer files electronically to another computer or to a printer. Software packages exist which are designed to speed up the transfer of files whilst also checking that no errors have been made during transfer. In order to make sure that a file transfer is made properly, the user will have to know where the data has to be sent (this may be an email address or a fax number) and to make sure that both of the devises are connected with one another. Once this has been established, the user will also have to name the file which needs to be transferred and then transfer the document, making sure that the connection is closed once the transfer has been completed.

Databases

Access to databases has become an integral part of most organisations' daily operations. Central databases provide a store of information which is continually updated, and many organisations need to be able to access this data at all times. This is particularly true of centrally-held data relating to travel arrangements, product or service availability and the reservation of accommodation. Individuals in remote locations can gain access to the most up-to-date information held at the central office, ensuring that they are working on the same information as everyone else in the organisation.

Describe protocols

In order for any electronic communication system to work, the sending machine and the receiving machine need to speak in the same language and to follow the same set of rules or **protocols**. These protocols ensure that all messages which are transmitted arrive at the correct destination, avoiding any errors and ensuring complete accuracy. This entails both the sender and the receiver agreeing on the parameters and protocols involved – a process often referred to as **hand-shaking** – and it means that the receiving machine understands what the sending machine is trying to do.

Baud rate

Simply, the **baud rate** is the speed at which data is transmitted. One baud is equal to one bit per second (BPS). Naturally, the sending and receiving machines must be set at the same baud rate. If this is not the case, then the data will be corrupted or perhaps not received at all. Telephone lines, for example, transmit at a baud rate of 19,200 bits per second.

Data bits

As you will no doubt be aware, computers hold all their information in the form of binary numbers. Six or eight **bits** make up a **byte**. Each letter comprises a pattern of 0s and 1s, so that all of the characters on a keyboard, including symbols, numbers and control codes, have their own specific string of binary numbers.

Flow controls

As you have probably noticed, any computer that you have used is able to transmit data much faster than your printer can handle. As a result, the printer needs to have a memory of its own, or **buffer**, where the printer will be able to store data transmitted by the computer, data which it will then process after it has completed the work it is currently doing. This is essential, as the receiver will not be able to function correctly if it is overloaded with data. Similarly, any transfer of information from one computer to another may also necessarily involve a delay whilst the receiving machine processes the information that it is currently handling.

Parity

In the American Standard Code for Information Interchange (ASCII), seven bits provide the 128 codes for all of the letters, codes and symbols on the keyboard. In order to ensure that data which is transmitted has not been changed or corrupted during transmission, it is essential that a **check digit** or **parity bit** be added to the end of the code. This allows both ends of the communication network to check that there is either an odd or an even number of 1 bits in each byte. If there is an even number of 1 bits, then the eighth bit is a 0. If there is an odd number of 1 bits, then the parity bit is a 1, and this will make an even number of 1 bits. This system works perfectly well provided that only 1 bit has been corrupted during transmission. If more than 1 bit has been corrupted, then the parity may be correct but the data may be wrong. Most computer systems will therefore use a more complex

cross-checking system in order to ensure that errors are identified and corrected.

Stop bits

The transmitter needs to tell the receiver when a byte or character begins and ends. If it were not for **stop bits**, then the receiver would just think that it had received an endless stream of binary data, which would be meaningless to it. Each byte has its usual eight bits which determine the character, preceded by a **start bit** and ending with a stop bit. Again, both the transmitter and the receiver need to know and recognise these start and stop bits.

Terminal emulation

For the vast majority of organisations, the terminals on each desk are simply ways in which the user can access the mainframe. They have no particular processing power of their own, and they therefore require a way in which they can access the processing power of the mainframe. In order to do this, each PC needs to emulate the standards required to communicate with the mainframe. This is achieved by having the correct software which has been coded to facilitate this connection.

4.1.3

Describe modes of communication

There are a number of different ways in which electronic communication can be carried out, dependent upon the type of cable used and the facilities available.

Duplex

This enables information to flow both ways, from sender to receiver and from receiver to sender, simultaneously. This is the most common form used for any type of interactive system or, more commonly, for a telephone conversation.

Half duplex

This connects both receiver and sender but allows only one party to communicate at a given time. In this way, the sender has first to transmit whilst the receiver receives, and then to switch to receive while the receiver in turn transmits (responds). **Half duplex** is the common way in which a Citizens' Band (CB) radio works, and is also typical of the communication between a mainframe and terminals.

Simplex

Simplex allows communication to be sent one way only, such as with a television broadcast or a radio transmission. There is no capacity for the receiver to send information back to the transmitter.

Parallel

Given the fact that each character or code from a keyboard consists of eight bits,

there needs to be a way in which this data can be transmitted or transported around the computer, or to another system. Usually, this is done with groups of 8, 16, 32 or 64 bits. All of the bits are transported along a series of separate parallel lines, or wires, which are known as a **bus**. In order to ensure that all of the bits arrive at the same time, **parallel transmission** is only really suitable for short distances. It is a quick way of transmitting data from the computer to a printer or a disk, but if the distance is longer than this, then parallel wires or lines are not really a viable choice.

Serial

For the transmission of data over greater distances, **serial transmission** is the only real alternative. Each bit of a byte is sent down the line and reassembled by the receiving machine at the other end. In order to do this, a chip will first convert the parallel transmission into a serial transmission and then allow it to be sent down the electronic communication line or wire.

Security requirements

For information on security requirements, see again Element 3.4.4.

4.2

Use an electronic communication system

student activity

In order to cover the second element of this unit, you will need to be observed transferring, receiving and storing electronic files and documents. By considering the following from the range statements, you can check to see whether or not you have covered all of the necessary areas from the previous two elements:

- *set up:* mode of communication, protocols, telephone numbers (see Element 4.1)
- *electronic system:* communications software, computer, modem, telephone network, facsimile (see Element 4.1)
- *accuracy checks:* echoing, parity checks (see Element 3.4)
- *security checks:* encryption, passwords, privileges, user identity (see Element 3.4).

4.3

Examine Computer Networks

4.3.1 Describe types of network and services available on networks

Perhaps without realising it, we all make extensive use of networks every day. Most telephone networks incorporate many of the features which we will be investigating in this element of the unit. In order to understand how the various networks operate, it is important to consider the ways in which the data is transferred through the network from computer to computer.

Data is transferred in a number of different ways and the visible signs of this are the sockets and the electronic cables. However, the process itself is rather more complicated. In order to transmit data through a telephone system, for example, the digital data needs to be transformed into Frequency Shifting Keys (FSK) signals.

This is because the telephone network is designed to cope with voice-based information. The technology used to do this is well-known and the modem (actually a modulator/demodulator) performs this operation. Modern computers will have modems built in to their systems, but older machines will require the modem to be fitted using the RS232 (or other serial) interface. Once the computer has been 'hooked up' to a network, via a modem, it is capable of sending any form of data, including text, visual images, moving pictures or speech. It is the modem that is physically connected to the network and it is the modem that links the computer to the network. The correct terminology labels the modem as a

DCE (data communications equipment) and the computer, printer or workstation as the DTE (data terminal equipment).

We now need to turn our attention to the fact that the modems may be in place, connected to the network, and the computers or printers are ready to send and receive data, but can they communicate with one another? Surely a modem needs to know whether it is sending or receiving? Simply speaking, modems are communicating with one another all of the time. This is achieved by a continuous stream of specially synchronised sounds (known as SYN codes) being sent and received all of the time, regardless of the fact that the system may not actually be in use by an operator.

When the data is sent, it is transferred with the assistance of the SYN codes. In other words, the link between the sender and the receiver is maintained throughout the transmission of the data. Even with long transmissions, the link is still maintained by the sender and the receiver including SYN codes. The data actually reaches the buffer of the receiver, and the receiver will send messages back to the sender if a data error has been identified. This vital synchronised link is often referred to as the protocols of the system.

The best known protocol is called the OSI (Open Systems Interconnection) model. It was designed specifically to get around the problem of different manufacturers of machinery and software creating their own protocols that were not understood, or could not understand other machinery and software made by a competitor. The OSI system is referred to as a layered model. This means that different parts of the overall system are capable of dealing with potential link and error problems at the level or layer of difficulty. In other words, by simplifying the whole of the model by breaking it down into layers, there is less chance that the communications link will fail. The idea is that the OSI model can standardise the communication link where necessary, from the complex aspects of a particular type of software to the more basic problems with the hardware and connections. The OSI model has seven layers, these are as follows:

1 *the application layer* – this is what the user actually sees on the application
2 *the presentation layer* – this aims to handle the different data formats passing along the communications link
3 *the session layer* – this decides which form of synchronisation and control it will employ to suit the communications link
4 *the transport layer* – this acts as the interface between the layers mentioned above and the three layers described below. In other words, it handles the actual arrival of the data at its destination
5 *the network layer* – this handles the switching and the routing of messages by establishing and then maintaining connections
6 *data-link layer* – this deals with the synchronisation, errors and transmission speed of the communication
7 *physical layer* – this handles the mechanics and electronics, ensuring that the physical connections are established and maintained.

The data is transported through the different layers of the system – the sender uses the application and the data works its way through the layers to the receiver, and then back up through the layers until it reaches the application being used by the receiver.

Multiplexing allows data to be carried for several DTEs at the same time. Alternatively, it can allow the user to use the system for a multitude of different uses. Although multiplexing is also known as MUX, it is better known as multi-tasking. This ability lies at the very heart of a complex and flexible network system. A system that has a MUX ability can handle communications from several different terminals which are sending and receiving data all at the same time. Typically, a MUX system will employ either a fibre-optic cable or a series of copper wires in order to facilitate the connections. At the end of each of the cables there will be a decoder (known as a demultiplexer) which can 'translate' the data back into a format which is understood by the terminal.

Digitisation is another means of sending several complex communications through a network. This system compresses the data being sent into 'packets' of information that are assembled and disassembled, as required, when they are sent or received.

Digitisation can greatly enhance the speed of the communications system and flexibility of the network.

Local area networks

A local area network (LAN) is an integrated communication system which connects a series of computers and peripherals together. This type of communication system is usually housed in a single site (hence local area) which allows different departments within the organisation to communicate freely and efficiently without producing vast amounts of paper-based materials. In most cases, there will be a mainframe computer used for routing and storing data and other files.

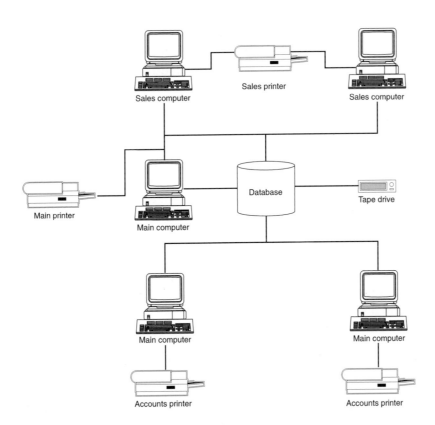

FIGURE 4.3.1 *Scapegoat's Local Area Network*

Being able to share information within the organisation is a distinct advantage and the LAN is seen by many organisations as a natural step forward from stand-alone personal computers. Having said this, a large number of organisations still manage with stand-alones, but they have the difficulty of having to back-up information as well as sharing it via discs.

F OCUS STUDY

Scapegoat's LAN system

When John Green and Emma Levy set up their new business they had little idea about computers, or the potential advantages that a LAN could offer them. Initially, they had operated the business from their home in London. When they started trading in alternative medicines and other green products, they worked solely by mail order using mailing lists that they had acquired from extensive market research, and other data gathering exercises at various conventions and exhibitions throughout the country. As the demand for their products increased, they realised that they would have to find new business premises, take on some staff and find some way in which they could computerise and streamline their stock control and ordering systems.

Having found a suitable building for the business and increased the number of staff to five, they began to analyse their current systems in order to work out what kind of computer system they would need. John and Emma had originally purchased two stand-alone computers – one to handle the stock control and the other to cope with the invoicing and ordering. John and Emma decided to set some time aside and work out exactly what they would need based on the following facts:

- most of their orders came in by telephone or by mail

- they needed to be able to inform each customer whether they had the item in stock, then to reserve that stock so that it was not sold to someone else
- all of their stock needed to be counted accurately so that they would be able to establish minimum stock levels and know precisely how much stock they had left at any one time
- ordered stock would need to be dispatched immediately, or held until the payment was received
- they would need to be able to create invoices and statements, credit levels and work out the VAT (if applicable) for the business customers.

They decided that they get rid of the manual systems that they had been using and invest in several PCs all linked on a LAN within the building. They believed that this would mean they would not need to hold large stocks of paper-based materials and filing systems, making the business far more cost-effective and efficient. In creating the LAN the business could share all of the information stored in the system and satisfy all of the needs identified above.

Wide area networks

A wide area network (WAN) is designed to link two or more computers or peripherals in remote locations. They have many of the same features as a LAN, but are more flexible and potentially more powerful as

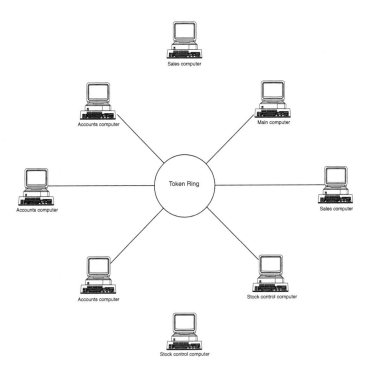

FIGURE 4.3.3 *A ring typology network*

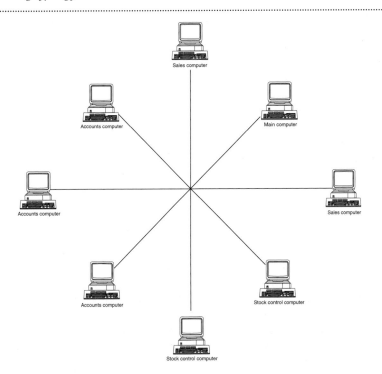

FIGURE 4.3.4 *A star typology network*

basis. This does mean, however, that the data transfer rates are relatively slow compared to other network typology options.

Mesh

The mesh system can be seen as a means of developing a network based on organic growth, rather than ripping out an existing system and replacing it completely. In this way, the interconnections between the workstation is, at best, rather haphazard and complex. Every workstation has to be physically connected to every other workstation in order to communicate and transmit data to them. The layouts of the overall system may be somewhat confused and prone to breakdowns and errors. Having said this, the mesh system is typical of the kind of configuration found in WAN systems where the access to

different stations and the multiple routing is an advantage.

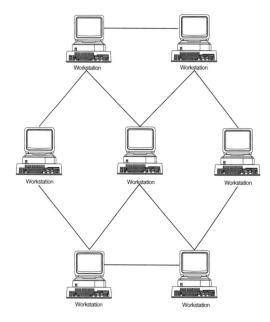

FIGURE 4.3.5 *A mesh typology network*

4.3.5 Describe security requirements for computer networks

User identity

In order to ensure that the network recognises the individual user and their right to use and access the data (and applications) on the network, each user will have to be given a user identity. This means that the user will have to input their user identity code (which may be a name or number or combination of both of these) before the network will allow them access to the files and the applications. The user identity system is often used in conjunction with a password and access rights that have been incorporated into the network's operating systems.

Password

Passwords are used to determine the actual identity of the user, regardless of the use of user identity codes or other means of filtering out unauthorised access to the network's systems. The user will have to input a code name or password (which is not displayed on the screen when it is keyed into the computer). This means that the network owner will know precisely who is logged on to the system, the duration of their use of the system and when they have logged off. Organisations running networks out to remote locations will be able to monitor precisely the activities of their employees or authorised network users.

Access rights

The employment of access rights and levels is a vital aspect of the security and management of a network. The organisation will attach a certain access right to particular user identities and passwords, and effectively block out access to certain areas of the network, applications and data. This is a means of being able to protect sensitive data and ensure that unauthorised individuals cannot tamper with, download or otherwise get access to confidential data. The access rights can also help the organisation to control the use of software applications.

Legal requirements

We have already considered the importance of the Data Protection Act in an earlier unit, but it is imperative that this consideration is re-emphasised here, particularly with reference to the right of disclosure of information held about individuals on a network system.

Network owners need to register their databases with the Data Protection Registrar just as any other owner of a database must do, but there are other legal implications which should be considered at this stage. Given the fact that access to the databases can be achieved via the network, the owner must ensure that access is only given to those who have a legitimate right to see that data. Confidentiality is therefore essential in order to ensure that information does not get into the wrong hands.

Other legislative considerations already mentioned elsewhere in this book include the copyright of the applications and the software used on the network, the health and safety aspects that are related to the use of computers and other hardware, and the considerations which revolve around the possible misuse of computers and the data stored on networks by individuals.

4.4

Use a computer network

student activity

To check that you understand how to use a computer network, your tutor will observe you carrying out a number of different procedures on the network, or you may be expected to keep a record of your activities in the form of a log book. In order to give you a clear idea as to the kind of things that you will need to cover and mention in such a log book, please refer to the following extracts from the range statements:

- *security procedures:* avoidance of data corruption, avoidance of data loss, copyright (data, software), log-in procedures, maintaining confidentiality
- *manage own files:* back up, copy, delete, file protection, move.

End test questions

1 A computer network which depends on a broadcast system is known as which of the following?

   a   a WAN
   b   electronic mail
   c   electronic noticeboards
   d   a LAN.

2 A computer network which is located within just one office location is known as which ONE of the following?

   a   a WAN
   b   electronic mail
   c   electronic noticeboards
   d   a LAN.

3 The term VHF refers to which ONE of the following?

   a   variable high frequency
   b   very high frequency
   c   very hollow frequency
   d   variable hollow frequency.

4 Microwaves are also known as SHF. Which ONE of the following does this stand for?

   a   super high frequency
   b   special high frequency
   c   specific high frequency
   d   standard high frequency.

5 Which ONE of the following is NOT a benefit of computer networks?

   a   central services
   b   shared resources
   c   teamworking
   d   improved software.

6 Which ONE of the following do data bits always carry?

   a   digital information
   b   parity checks
   c   start codes
   d   stop codes.

7 In order for any electronic communication system to work, the sending machine and the receiving

machine need to speak in the same language and follow the same set of protocols. Which ONE of the following is NOT associated with protocols?

a   ensuring that messages are transmitted and arrive at the correct destination
b   avoiding any errors
c   ensuring complete accuracy
d   a spellchecking facility.

8   Which ONE of the following describes the speed at which data is transmitted?

a   the baud rate
b   the data bits
c   the flow controls
d   the parity.

9   A parity bit allows the data receiver to do which ONE of the following?

a   ensure that there are eight bits
b   identify any data errors
c   identify start and stop codes
d   recognise an odd bit.

10   Which ONE of the following is it necessary to identify when setting up an electronic mail system?

a   the printer codes
b   the telephone exchange location
c   the system password
d   the modem protocols.

11   When a message is received using an electronic mail system, which ONE of the following does the software update?

a   a system of parity checks
b   a system of privileges
c   a list of electronic mail addresses
d   a list of user passwords.

12   One way of ensuring that information which is being transmitted using electronic mail is safe and secure is to use which ONE of the following?

a   a password
b   codes
c   privileges
d   encryption.

13   The network facility which allows the users to leave messages for and receive messages from other users is known as which ONE of the following?

a   electronic mail
b   video conferencing
c   bulletin board
d   wide area network.

14   If the network facility allowed the users to use real-time communications, which ONE of the following would it be called?

a   electronic mail
b   video conferencing
c   bulletin board
d   wide area network.

15   If a building society regularly sent information from one branch to another, which ONE of the following network facilities would it be using?

a   electronic mail
b   video conferencing
c   bulletin board
d   file transfer.

16   Which ONE of the following is the MOST essential piece of hardware for a network in order for it to function adequately?

a   a printer
b   a modem
c   a dumb terminal
d   a network card.

17   If a network has four work stations and only one printer, which ONE of the following must be used?

a   a file server

b   a print server
c   a VDU
d   a hard drive.

18 Government legislation affects a great deal of computer networks. Which ONE of the following is particularly affected?

a   protocols
b   printers
c   health and safety
d   security.

19 Which ONE of the following aspects of networks is particularly affected by legislation?

a   communications
b   confidentiality of data
c   security
d   identification of user.

20 Which ONE of the following is an access right?

a   user ID
b   password
c   read only
d   random access.

21 For the transmission of data over greater distances, serial transmission is the only real alternative. Which ONE of the following is true of serial transmission?

a   a chip will first convert the parallel transmission into a serial transmission
b   a chip will convert the serial transmission into a parallel transmission
c   a chip will convert the data
d   a chip will convert the bus.

22 Given the fact that each character or code from a keyboard consists of eight bits, there needs to be a way in which the data can be transmitted or transported around the computer, or to another system. Usually, this is done with groups of which ONE of the following?

a   8, 16, 32, 64 bits
b   10, 12, 14, 16 bits
c   2, 4, 6, 8 bits
d   20, 40, 60, 80 bits.

23 All of the bits are transported along a series of separate parallel lines, or which ONE of the following?

a   serial
b   parity
c   bus
d   transmitters.

24 It is possible to avoid the loss of data due to corruption during file transfer by using which ONE of the following?

a   passwords
b   verification
c   validation
d   backups.

25 Which TWO of the following are file management activities?

1   setting up a new user
2   copying files
3   moving files
4   setting file access rights.
    a   1 and 2
    b   2 and 3
    c   3 and 4
    d   1 and 4.

Glossary

Applications software Software which is used for a specific purpose. This could be word processing, desktop publishing, spreadsheets or databases. Integrated software provides all of these in one package.

Attribute A single data item which represents an individual property of the object (entity) used in the database.

Batch processing A schedule for the compete processing over time of a collection of jobs or materials.

Bitmap graphics A graphic image or test formed by a pattern of dots or **pixels**.

Buffer A temporary storage area for information which is being transmitted between different components of a computer system.

Bus An electrical connection with a computer system allowing data to pass from one component to another.

Byte Usually eight bits of information (a unit) handled by a computer system.

CAD Computer-aided design.

CAM Computer-aided manufacture.

Control procedure The program created to operate a process control system. It is designed to read input data and then process and send this data.

Control system A computer system which automatically controls a process by sensing the need to vary the output.

Control unit The functional part of a computer which takes instructions individually and interprets them.

Data storage The ways in which data and information are stored. This could be on tape or on disk.

Database An organised collection of data, stored in files.

Database report The production of output from a database.

Default A configuration of software or hardware according to a standard set of values.

DOS Disk-operating system.

Electronic mail (email) The use of a computer network to transmit mail electronically by use of a 'mailbox'.

Facsimile transmission An exact copy of a document transmitted (usually in digital form) via a telecommunication link.

Feedback The process whereby a part of the output is fed back into the input to enable certain actions to be taken to reduce or increase future output.

Field The part of a database record which allows the storage of a particular piece of data (an **attribute**).

File A collection of related **records**.

File protection Enables a user to impose certain restrictions on **files** and sub-directories for other users, e.g. 'read only'.

File server The computer which contains the network software for other stations on a **network** to access.

Footer A standard line of print which a computer is instructed to insert at the foot of every page (or of selected pages).

Gaming The use of software to model a situation.

Graphic user interface An **operating system** which allows a user to produce graphic material.

Header A standard line of text which the computer is instructed to insert at the top of every page (or of selected pages).

Hypothesis testing Using computer models (e.g. spreadsheets) to test 'what if' queries for possible situations.

Icons Symbols which appear on the screen and represent an option for the **program** being used.

Importing The transfer of data from a **file** into existing files or documents.

Index file A file within a **database** which allows quick reference to the records in a pre-set order.

Input devices The means by which information or data can be inputted into the computer, e.g. keyboard, mouse.

Integrated package Software which provides several packages in one, e.g. word processing, spreadsheet, database and graphics packages.

Key One of the **attributes** of an entity on which an index has been created.

Local area network This allows the sharing of data, software and equipment resources. The computers are connected by cable, and are usually located in a single building or site.

Macro A program written using applications-software tools to automate a sequence of **keystrokes** or events.

Magnetic strip reader Used for automatic data collection, e.g. automated tills and credit cards used for the electronic transfer of funds.

Mail merge Merging a standard letter with a datafile of names and addresses. Each letter's text is the same but is addressed to different people.

Main processor unit This includes the following: **motherboard, controller boards**, special processors, input and output ports.

Micro-computer A system of both hardware and software which comprises the **main processor unit**, keyboard, **VDU** and peripheral units.

Model A **software** representation of a real situation which can be used for analysis purposes.

Modelling Analysis of a situation by using a computer model.

Modem Allows the transference of information from one computer to another via a telephone line, e.g. for **electronic mail**.

Operating system Software program providing the environment in which applications programs can be used.

Output devices These include the **VDU, printer**, plotter, controller devices, and speech and audio devices.

Permanent storage Storage of data on **ROM**.

Pixel The smallest element which can be displayed on a video display screen.

Prediction The use of computer **models** to forecast a situation.

Primary key The **attribute** used as a primary and unique index key for an **entity**.

Primary storage The storing of data and instructions in **ROM** and **RAM**.

Printer The **output device** which produces characters or graphic symbols on **hard copy**.

Printer server The computer which contains the printer server software for a **local area network**, and which controls the printer queue.

Process control The automated control of a processing plant where input flow and control are regulated by output measurements.

Program A set of instructions to the computer which are structured to meet a given set of needs.

Proofreading The visual checking of content to ensure accuracy and correct layout and style.

Quality control The use of a **process control** system to measure the quality of products.

RAM Random access memory. Information saved on RAM is lost when power is switched off.

Record A collection of related data items.

ROM Read only memory. Information is not lost when power is switched off. ROM is not **volatile**.

Searching Searching data to locate a given value or string of characters.

Security Controlled access to **networks** and the provision of back-up, virus protection, audit trails, and theft- and copyright-protection systems.

Selecting The searching for and extraction of data which matches the search requirement.

Sensor A device which outputs electrical signals when changes occur in its environment.

Simulation A software representation of a real situation which may be used for analysis or training purposes.

Software The **programs** which allow a computer to operate.

Software facilities Contained within the software, they enable the user to carry out tasks, e.g. **macros, mail merge**.

Sorting The putting of data into numerical or alphabetical order.

Special fields Used in databases to contain special data, e.g. date, time.

Stand-alone computer A system complete in itself, requiring no other devices for it to operate, e.g. **micro-computers**, when not connected to any **network**.

Template A standardised document layout or screen format, e.g. a memorandum or letterhead. It can also refer to overlays for keyboard keys, to indicate their action when used with a particular application.

Temporary storage Usually magnetic tapes and disks, or laser disks and CD-disks.

Transaction processing A data-processing system which handles one transaction at a time.

User The person who is currently accessing information through information technology systems.

Validation Checking a data entry to confirm both that it is within the acceptable range and that it is not incomplete.

VDU Visual display unit, or screen.

Vector graphic A graphic image where the elements are defined using geometry which enables scaling without loss of resolution.

Verification The checking of date entries for accuracy.

Voice recognition Allows a user to input information simply by speaking.

Volatile Subject to change: related to computer memory, it means data is lost when the power is switched off.

Window An area of the computer screen which is dedicated to a particular function. Several 'windows' may be available at any one time on the screen.

Workstation The term could be used to described a **stand-alone computer** or a terminal on a **network**, or simply the desk on which a computer is housed.

Index